Dating at Nervous-System Speed

A Trauma-Aware Guide to Dating Someone with PTSD or CPTSD Without Rushing, Losing Yourself, or Walking on Eggshells

Lawrence Simeon Mooney

Copyright

A note on what this book is, and is not. This book offers information, ideas, and practical tools for people dating someone who lives with post-traumatic stress. It is not therapy, medical advice, or a substitute for care from a licensed professional. It does not diagnose anyone, and it will not teach you to diagnose your partner. If you are worried about your safety or your partner's safety, contact a qualified professional or, in the United States, call or text the 988 Suicide and Crisis Lifeline.

About the people in these pages. Every person named in this book is a fictional composite. The names are drawn from a fixed set chosen for that purpose, and the stories are assembled from patterns common in trauma-aware dating, not from any single real person. Any resemblance to a real individual is coincidental. The point of these composites is not to show you clean before-and-after transformations. Real early relationships include false starts, partial wins, and clear-eyed exits, and the stories here reflect that.

First Edition

ISBN; 979-8-90678-213-7

Staten House

Table of Contents

Preface

Public understanding of trauma has advanced considerably in recent years. The eleventh revision of the World Health Organization's International Classification of Diseases now recognizes complex post-traumatic stress as a distinct condition, and a growing shelf of books helps couples live with the aftermath of trauma inside a committed relationship. Almost all of that guidance assumes a shared history worth protecting, a marriage, a family, years already built. Very little of it speaks to the person who is still deciding whether to build anything at all.

Trauma-aware dating is the practice this book defines and teaches. It is the work of forming a new relationship with someone who lives with post-traumatic stress or complex post-traumatic stress, at the early stage when trust is still forming and the future is still open. It is not couples therapy, which repairs an established bond, and it is not clinical treatment, which belongs to the survivor and their own care. It is something more ordinary and, for many people, more confusing: how to court, pace, and assess a relationship whose rhythms do not match the scripts most of us were handed.

The difficulty is that those scripts fail quietly. A partner at this stage often cannot tell whether a slow reply signals fading interest or a nervous system seeking rest, or whether sudden distance after a close evening calls for patience or for a firm boundary. Without a framework, people default to two errors. They over-accommodate, reshaping themselves around a partner's symptoms until little of themselves remains, or they misread every difficulty as danger and leave good relationships for being imperfect. Both errors come from the same absence, a missing map for unfamiliar terrain.

This book supplies one. It organizes the early relationship around a set of named principles, each a practical tool the reader can apply within the week, and it builds toward a clear decision framework for the hardest question of all, whether to stay and build or to leave with care. Along the way it teaches when to ask about a partner's history and when to wait, what to do when something is triggered without taking on the role of therapist, how to keep consent alive in physical intimacy, and how to tell a red flag from a trauma response without diagnosing anyone. The aim is a relationship paced in a way both people can sustain, chosen on purpose rather than fallen into.

A few plain limits close this preface. This book does not diagnose, it does not treat, and it does not promise that any particular relationship will succeed or should. It offers information, structure, and judgment rather than guarantees. What it provides is a clearer way to think, and to decide, about building intimacy with someone whose trust becomes safe more slowly than most.

Introduction: The Pace No One Taught You

You met someone you like. Maybe more than like. And somewhere in the early glow, you learned something that reorganized how you read every text, every quiet evening, every time they got close and then went still. They have post-traumatic stress. Or complex post-traumatic stress. Or they used the word trauma once, carefully, and you have been turning it over ever since.

Here is what I want to say before anything else. The problem in front of you is almost never the trauma itself. The problem is that no one taught you the pace. You were handed the ordinary scripts for dating, the ones about playing it cool and matching energy and knowing after three dates whether this is going somewhere, and none of those scripts fit. So you improvise. You reassure too much, or you go quiet to be safe, or you read a slow reply as a verdict. You start managing a relationship you have barely begun to build.

This is a dating book, and that word matters. Most books written for the partners of people with trauma are written for couples with a shared life, a mortgage, children, years of history to protect. Aphrodite Matsakis wrote a good one for that reader. So did others. Their questions are how to repair, how to endure, how to stay. Your questions are different and, in some ways, harder, because you have not decided yet. When do you ask about the trauma? How much are you owed? How fast should you merge your lives? When is sudden distance a reason to be patient, and when is it a reason to walk away? Nobody wrote the book for the person standing exactly where you are standing. So I did.

I am not going to romanticize trauma, and I am not going to treat your partner like a problem to be solved. Both moves fail you. Trauma does not lower a person's worth, and it does not raise your obligation to abandon your own needs. What trauma can do, sometimes, is change the speed at which trust becomes safe to extend. That is the whole idea behind the title. You are learning to date at a pace your partner's nervous system, and your own, can actually tolerate, and, just as important, a pace you both choose on purpose rather than fall into.

A few candid promises about what is ahead. You will get a way to think about disclosure that treats your partner's story as theirs to give, not yours to extract. You will get a practice for the silent hours between texts that ends the spiral without pretending you feel nothing. You will get language for the pattern where closeness is followed by distance, and a clear line between patience and tolerating harm. You will get a plain, non-clinical way to respond when something gets triggered on a date. You will get a consent-centered approach to touch and sex that keeps both of you free to stop. And you will get the two hardest tools of all: a way to tell a red flag from a trauma response without diagnosing anyone, and a way to decide whether this relationship is actually worth building.

One thing I will keep returning to, because it is easy to lose. You are not your partner's therapist. You cannot regulate someone else's nervous system, and any book that promises you can is selling you a job you should refuse. Your work is smaller and more sustainable than that. Notice the pace. Communicate plainly. Keep your own life. Stay truthful about what is present between you. Decide.

You do not have to read this in order, though the early chapters build a foundation the later ones lean on. Start where your pain is loudest. If the thing keeping you up is a two-day silence, go to the chapter on silence. If it is the question of whether to stay, the last chapter is waiting for you. Wherever you begin, come back to the frame, because the frame is what keeps you steady when the relationship gets confusing, which it will.

Let us begin where every trauma-aware relationship has to begin, with the difference between changing pace and lowering worth.

Chapter 1: Trauma Changes Pace, Not Worth

Avelis noticed the pause before she noticed anything else. She was thirty-one, three weeks into something with a man named Lorien, and everything about the early dates had been easy in the way good things are easy, until the night he told her, in the kitchen, over the last of the wine, that he had been diagnosed with post-traumatic stress two years earlier. He said it plainly. Then he stopped, and the pause sat between them like a third person at the table, and Avelis felt the whole evening reorganize itself around that one sentence. She heard herself say, "Thank you for telling me," which was true, and then she spent the next four days quietly rewriting her memory of every moment they had shared, looking for the trauma she had missed, treating him, without meaning to, as a slightly different and more fragile person than the one she had actually been laughing with all month.

That reflex, the one that takes a single fact and quietly downgrades a whole human being, is where trauma-aware dating goes wrong before it even starts. So this chapter is about a frame, not a technique. Get the frame right and the tools in the rest of the book land where they should. Get it wrong and even good tools turn into careful, exhausting management of a person who never asked to be managed.

What the words actually mean

Let us start with the vocabulary, because you are probably carrying a mix of accurate knowledge and internet folklore, and the folklore causes trouble. Post-traumatic stress disorder, in plain terms, is a set of persistent responses that can follow exposure to an event that was extremely threatening or horrific. The core clusters are re-experiencing the event in the present, avoiding reminders of it, and a lasting sense of current threat, the nervous system staying oriented toward danger even when the danger is over.

Complex post-traumatic stress, or CPTSD, is the same core plus something more. It tends to follow prolonged or repeated trauma, often beginning early in life and often at the hands of people who were supposed to provide care. Judith Herman first described this pattern in her 1992 book *Trauma and Recovery*, arguing that chronic betrayal inside relationships produces wounds single-incident models did not capture (Herman, 1992). The World Health Organization eventually formalized it. In the eleventh revision of the International Classification of Diseases, CPTSD is a recognized diagnosis defined as the three PTSD clusters plus three additional features grouped as disturbances in self-organization: difficulty regulating emotion, a persistently negative self-concept, and difficulty feeling close in relationships (World Health Organization, 2019; Cloitre et al., 2018). Researchers have tested that structure across many countries and found it holds up, with the PTSD and CPTSD profiles separating cleanly in most studies (Brewin et al., 2017; Shevlin et al., 2018).

Here is a distinction worth knowing if you are in the United States. CPTSD appears in the World Health Organization's system, but it is not a separate diagnosis in the American manual, the DSM-5-TR (American Psychiatric Association, 2022). This is not a contradiction so much as two committees drawing a line in slightly different places. What it means for you, practically, is that your partner may describe themselves as having complex PTSD even though a given American clinician might record their diagnosis differently. That gap is about paperwork and classification systems, not about whether their experience is real.

Why any of this matters on a Tuesday

You are not going to quiz your partner on symptom clusters, and you should not try. The reason the vocabulary matters is that it gives you a way to hold what you are seeing without inventing explanations. When your partner goes quiet after a hard conversation, or flinches at a sound you did not notice, or needs a full day alone after a wonderful evening, you have two options. You can narrate it, filling the silence with a story about what it means about you and about them. Or you can hold it lightly, as one data point, and wait. The vocabulary helps you wait, because it reminds you that a lasting sense of threat is a known feature of a known condition, not a secret message about your worth or theirs.

What trauma tends to change, in a relationship, is pace. Closeness that would feel simply good to one nervous system can feel like exposure to another. Reviews of the research on trauma and relationships consistently find that symptoms of avoidance and emotional numbing are the ones most tied to relationship strain, because they pull a person back from the very intimacy the relationship is built on (National Center for PTSD, n.d.; Campbell & Renshaw, 2012). Notice the word. Pace. Not capacity, not worth, not whether love is possible. The speed at which trust becomes safe to extend can be slower, and it can be uneven, faster on Monday than on Thursday for reasons neither of you will always be able to name.

The Pace Principle

This is the idea the whole book rests on, so I will name it and we will keep coming back to it. The Pace Principle: trauma can change the speed at which a relationship becomes safe, but it never changes the worth of the person you are dating, and it never obligates you to abandon your own pace to match theirs. Two people, two nervous systems, one shared speed that you negotiate on purpose. That is the work.

Read the second half of that sentence again, because people skip it. Trauma-aware dating is not a one-way accommodation where you shrink yourself around your partner's edges. That version burns out fast, and it is unfair to both of you, because it turns you into a caretaker and turns them into a patient, and neither of those is a person you can build a real relationship with. The pace is shared. Your comfort counts. Your need for a reply, your desire for closeness, your limits, all of it stays on the table.

Avelis found the frame slowly, and not gracefully. Her first instinct, those four days of quiet rewriting, was to become gentler, more careful, a softer version of herself she thought Lorien needed. It did not go well. He noticed the shift and read it, accurately, as pity, and pulled back, which frightened her, which made her more careful still. They almost lost the thing in the first month, not because of his trauma but because of her response to it. What turned it around was ordinary and a little anticlimactic. She said, over coffee, "I think I have been treating you like glass since you told me, and I do not actually want to do that, and I am not sure what you want either." He exhaled. He said he had spent two years being handled and had hoped she might just keep being the person who made him laugh. So she did. The trauma did not go anywhere. But it stopped being the center of gravity.

The rule that keeps you clear-eyed: you do not diagnose

There is a temptation, once you know your partner has trauma, to become an amateur clinician. You start reading everything through the lens of symptoms. He was short with the waiter, that is his hypervigilance. She did not text back, that is her avoidance. You build a private diagnostic file, and it feels like understanding, but it is actually a subtle form of control, because a person you have fully explained is a person you have stopped actually listening to.

So here is a rule I will ask you to hold for the entire book. You do not diagnose your partner, and you do not attribute every behavior to their trauma. You are not qualified to, and more importantly, it is not useful. Bessel van der Kolk's work on how trauma lives in the body has helped many people, but even the best clinical knowledge in someone else's hands, aimed at a partner rather than a patient, tends to produce more confusion than clarity (van der Kolk, 2014). People in trauma support communities say this bluntly: a supporter who tries to understand every mechanism usually ends up more lost, because a partner's job is to support and to stay truthful, not to explain.

Not everything your partner does is trauma. Some of it is personality. Some of it is preference. Some of it is a bad mood, or a hard week, or a genuine incompatibility between the two of you that has nothing to do with anyone's history. When you file every behavior under trauma, you lose the ability to tell these apart, and telling them apart is exactly what you will need later, when you have to decide whether something is a response worth patience or a pattern worth leaving. Keeping the categories separate now is what makes that decision possible then.

A word about the word "nervous system"

You will notice I have used the phrase nervous system a few times, and it is in the title of this book, so I owe you some candor about it. The language of regulation and nervous systems has become popular, and it is popular for a good reason. It gives people a way to talk about reactions that are faster than thought, the flinch, the shutdown, the sudden flood, without turning them into moral failures. When your partner freezes, it is genuinely useful to understand that a body can react to a memory as if it were a present threat, below the level of choice.

But popular language gets slippery, and this one has gotten very slippery. There is a version of it floating around now that explains everything and therefore explains nothing. In that version, every mood is dysregulation, every disagreement is a trigger, every ordinary human limit is a nervous system problem, and, worst of all, one person is supposed to be able to regulate another person's body through sheer attuned presence. I want to draw a firm line under that last idea in particular. You cannot regulate your partner's nervous system. You can be a calm, steady presence, and calm can be contagious in small ways, but their internal state is theirs, produced by their body and their history and, ideally, their own support and their own practice. A book that promises you the power to soothe another adult's physiology on demand is handing you a responsibility no one can actually meet, and setting you up to feel like a failure every time your partner has a hard day you did not cause and cannot fix.

So use the language the way you would use any useful tool, and put it down when it stops helping. When it reminds you that a reaction is fast, bodily, and not a comment on your worth, keep it. When it starts turning your partner into a bundle of symptoms, or turning you into their designated regulator, set it aside and come back to plainer words. He needed space tonight. She was overwhelmed and could not say why. I do not fully understand this yet, and I do not have to. Plain language keeps you grounded in a way that clinical language, in the wrong hands, quietly does not.

Keeping the categories separate cuts both ways, and it is worth seeing the other edge of it now. A reader I will call Caelan, twenty-eight, spent five months excusing a partner's cutting remarks and disappearing acts as trauma responses, because the partner had a real and serious history and Vaelan did not want to be the person who punished someone for being wounded. The frame, when he finally applied it, did not tell him the remarks were fine. It told him the opposite. Trauma explained where the behavior might have come from. It did not make the behavior acceptable, and it did not obligate him to keep absorbing it. He left, carefully and without cruelty, and he was right to. I put this here, in the first chapter, so the frame does not get mistaken for a doctrine of endless patience. Understanding a behavior and accepting a behavior are two different acts, and this book will keep them apart the whole way through.

What is yours to carry, and what is not

The frame has one more piece, and it is the piece that protects you. There is a line between supporting someone and taking responsibility for their internal state, and trauma-aware dating asks you to find that line early and stand on it. You can be kind, patient, and steady. You cannot regulate another person's nervous system, calm their body for them, or love them out of a condition. Anyone who tells you otherwise is describing a job that does not exist, and taking that job is how people lose themselves in these relationships.

Try this, this week. Take a sheet of paper and draw a line down the middle. On the left, write the things that are genuinely yours to carry in this relationship: your candor, your patience within reason, your willingness to communicate, your own limits, your own pace. On the right, write the things that are not yours: your partner's healing, their moods, their history, the speed of their recovery, the work only they and their own support can do. When you feel the pull to fix, manage, or rescue this week, look at the sheet. Anything on the right side, hand it back, gently, to the person it belongs to. Not coldly. Just accurately.

Be concrete when you make the list, because vague lists do nothing. On the left, real entries look like this: whether I reply openly instead of strategically, whether I say when a plan does not work for me, whether I stay curious instead of assuming, how fast I let my own life get absorbed. On the right, real entries look like this: whether he sleeps tonight, whether her mood lifts by the weekend, how quickly the flashbacks fade, whether therapy is working. The test for which column something belongs in is simple. If you are the only one who can do it, it is yours. If it lives inside your partner's body or history or recovery, it is theirs, no matter how much you love them and how badly you want to reach in and fix it. The list is not a one-time exercise. It is a thing you return to on the hard nights, when the pull to rescue is strongest and your judgment is weakest.

Avelis kept a version of that list on her phone for a while. The night she stopped treating Lorien like glass, she was really just moving one item from the left column, where she had wrongly filed it, over to the right, where it had always belonged. His trauma was never hers to carry. The pace between them, though, that was shared, and shared things you can actually work with. That is where we are going next: the first real decision the pace asks of you, which is when to ask about the story, and when to wait.

Chapter 2: When To Ask, When To Wait

How much of someone's story are you owed on a third date? Sit with the question for a second before you answer, because the reflex answer, the one that says a real connection means full disclosure, is exactly the reflex that gets trauma-aware dating into trouble in its first month.

Vaelan, thirty-four, learned this the hard way from the other side of it. He had met someone he liked, and he knew she had a difficult history because she had said so, once, in passing. He decided that caring about her meant understanding her, and that understanding her meant knowing what had happened. So he asked. Not cruelly, just directly, over dinner on their fourth date: "You mentioned some hard stuff earlier. What happened to you?" She went pale, gave him a flat two-sentence summary, and then was different for the rest of the night, polite and far away. They had two more dates and then she stopped replying. Vaelan spent weeks convinced he had done something monstrous. He had not done something monstrous. He had done something common, which is to treat closeness as a key that unlocks a person's worst memories on his schedule rather than hers.

The story belongs to the person who lived it

Start here, because everything in this chapter grows from it. Your partner's trauma is their story, not shared property that dating entitles you to access. Liking someone, sleeping with someone, even loving someone does not create a right to the details of the worst thing that ever happened to them. Those details are theirs to offer, in their words, on their timeline, or to keep. This is not them being withholding. It is them being a person with a boundary, which is precisely the kind of person you want to be dating.

This reframes the whole question. The question is not when do I get to ask. The question is how do I make it safe for them to tell me, if and when they want to, and how do I stay comfortable not knowing in the meantime. Those are very different questions, and they produce very different behavior. The first turns you into an interrogator. The second turns you into someone worth confiding in.

There is real research underneath this, not just etiquette. Studies of couples affected by trauma have found that how much and what kind of trauma disclosure helps a relationship is genuinely complicated, not a simple more-is-better line. One study of military couples found that trauma symptoms predicted lower relationship quality mainly when disclosure was low to moderate, and that pattern did not hold in couples with high disclosure, which sounds like a case for asking more (Monk & Nelson Goff, 2014). But the same body of work makes clear that disclosure helps when it arrives on a foundation of trust, and lands badly when it is pulled out ahead of that foundation (Monson & Fredman, 2012). Sharing intimate thoughts and feelings is central to closeness, yes, but it is a process that has to match the depth of the relationship it is happening inside (Cook et al., 2004). Timing is not a detail. Timing is most of it.

The Open Door Rule

Here is the principle for this chapter. The Open Door Rule: your job is to leave the door open, not to push it open. You make it clear, through how you respond to the small things, that you are someone who can be told hard things without flinching or fixing or making it about you. Then you wait, and you let your partner decide whether and when to walk through.

Leaving the door open is mostly about how you handle the low-stakes disclosures, the ones that come before the big ones. When your partner mentions, lightly, that they do not do well with loud crowds, and you say "good to know, thanks for telling me" and then quietly adjust the plan without a fuss, you have just shown them what happens when they tell you something true. You have shown them it is safe. That single, small, non-dramatic response does more to make eventual deeper disclosure possible than any number of earnest invitations to open up. People do not open up because you asked them to. They open up because they watched how you handled the last thing and concluded you could handle the next thing.

Pushing the door open looks like Vaelan's dinner question. It looks like "you can tell me anything, you know." It looks like a meaningful silence after they mention something hard, a silence engineered to make them fill it. It looks like following up a small disclosure with "and what else?" All of these communicate that you are waiting to be given the trauma, and that waiting, however warmly intended, is pressure. Pressure is the one thing that reliably keeps the door shut.

When they tell you too much, too soon

The opposite problem is just as real, and this book would be misleading if it only warned you against asking. Sometimes a person shares a great deal of heavy, unprocessed pain very early, before there is any foundation to hold it. It can happen over text before a first date, or on the first date itself. When it does, you are left feeling drained and strangely responsible, as if you have been handed something you did not agree to carry.

This has a name in dating conversations now, and the name is trauma dumping, and I want to use it carefully, because it can be said with contempt and I do not mean it that way. The distinction that matters is not the heaviness of what is shared. It is whether it is an invitation into connection or a discharge onto whoever is in front of them. Healthy vulnerability tends to check in, to gauge your comfort, to leave room for you to be a person too. Premature unloading tends to bring relief to the person sharing and leave the listener feeling like an unpaid therapist. The timing, the absence of any built trust, is what makes it a signal worth noticing rather than a moment of intimacy.

So what do you do in the moment, without being cold and without signing up to carry it? You acknowledge the person without taking the job. Something like: "That sounds really heavy, and I can tell it matters. I hope you have good support for it, someone who is trained for this."

That sentence does three things at once. It honors what they shared. It does not pretend you are the right container for it this early. And it gently points toward the kind of support that actually helps, which is not a person they met last week. You can be warm and still keep your feet. Those are not opposites.

Isoren, twenty-nine, had to practice this. Her instinct, when a new partner unloaded a lifetime of pain on their second date, was to rise to it, to prove her devotion by absorbing all of it and offering to be everything. She did that for about three weeks and then found herself exhausted, resentful, and cast in a role she had never auditioned for. What she needed was not to be harder. It was to be candid earlier. When she finally said, kindly, "I care about you and I am not able to be your only support for something this big," the relationship did not end. It got more real. He was, it turned out, relieved to be treated like a partner instead of a patient, which is a pattern you will see again in this book.

Getting comfortable with not knowing

There is a piece of this that is entirely your own work, and no amount of good behavior toward your partner replaces it. You have to get comfortable not knowing. The pull to ask, to gather the whole story, is often less about your partner and more about your own discomfort with uncertainty. Not knowing feels unstable. The mind wants the full picture so it can stop bracing. And so asking, which looks like care, is sometimes really a way of soothing your own anxiety at your partner's expense.

Notice that in yourself, because it changes what you do. When you feel the urge to ask rise, pause and ask yourself a quieter question first. Do I need to know this to make a good decision right now, or do I just want to stop feeling uncertain? Almost always, in the early weeks, the truthful answer is the second one. You do not need your partner's trauma history to decide whether you enjoy their company, whether they treat you well, whether you want a fifth date. You need very little information to make the only decisions that are actually in front of you this early. The rest, the deep history, is not decision-relevant yet, and treating it as urgent is a habit of anxiety, not a requirement of the relationship.

This matters because your ability to sit with not knowing is one of the things that makes you safe to confide in. A person who cannot tolerate uncertainty telegraphs it. They ask a little too eagerly, they hover, they seem to need the story. A person who is genuinely comfortable not knowing gives off a different signal, one that says there is no rush, I am not going anywhere, tell me when you tell me. That signal, more than any words, is what eventually opens the door.

Disclosures that arrive by text, and other awkward channels

Not every disclosure comes across a candlelit table. Some of it arrives by text at eleven at night, or in a long message the morning after a good date, or in a nervous rush while you are doing something else entirely. The channel can make it harder to respond well, because a heavy thing sent by text can feel like it demands an immediate, perfect reply, and there is no perfect reply waiting in you at eleven at night.

You are allowed to slow it down. A disclosure does not obligate an instant response equal in weight to what was shared. It is completely fine to write back something warm and brief, and to save the real conversation for when you are together and present. "Thank you for trusting me with that. I want to talk about it properly, not over text. Can we when I see you Thursday?" That is not avoidance. It is respect, for the size of what they shared and for your own need to be a whole person rather than an always-on responder. The same tiered logic applies. Meet the disclosure at the tier the moment can actually hold, and let the deeper conversation happen where it can be held well.

Tiered sharing, in both directions

The practical model that ties this together is simple. Think of disclosure as tiered, arriving in layers that match the trust you have actually built, rather than all at once. Early on, a person might share the fact of a hard history without the contents. Later, the shape of it. Later still, if the relationship earns it, the details. Each tier is an offer, and each offer is a small test of whether the relationship can hold a little more. This works in both directions. It is how you want to receive your partner's story, and it is how you should share your own, because you have a history too, and dumping yours early does the same damage.

The myth that not asking means not caring

I want to name the belief that makes all of this hard, because until you name it, it runs you. The belief is that not asking about your partner's trauma means you do not care, that a truly loving partner would want to know everything and would ask. It sounds right. It is backwards. Wanting to know everything is often about your own need to feel close and in control of the picture. Being willing to not know, to let your partner keep the pace of their own story, is the more loving act, because it puts their comfort above your curiosity.

Isoren, again, is a good example of how this can go either way. In her next relationship she overcorrected. Having learned not to absorb everything, she swung to asking nothing at all, ever, and treating any mention of the past as a landmine to be tiptoed around. Her partner eventually told her the silence felt like avoidance, like she did not want to know him. The Open Door Rule is not the closed door rule. Leaving the door open means being visibly available, warm, unhurried, and unafraid, so that your partner knows they can walk through whenever they choose. It does not mean pretending their history does not exist. Isoren found the middle on her third try, which is worth saying plainly, because these skills are learned across relationships and false starts, not perfected in one.

The balance you are looking for is a kind of relaxed readiness. You are not extracting, and you are not avoiding. You are simply the sort of person who can be told things, and who does not need to be told things to keep showing up. That combination, availability without demand, is rarer than it sounds and more attractive than any amount of intensity.

Here is your action for this week, and it is a listening exercise, not a talking one. The next time your partner tells you something small and true, anything, a preference, a discomfort, a minor fear, do three things and nothing more. Thank them plainly. Adjust something visibly, if there is anything to adjust. And ask nothing further. Resist every urge to follow up, to dig, to say you can tell them anything. Just show them, with your calm and your lack of drama, what it is like to be heard by you. Do that reliably with the small things, and the door to the larger things will open on its own timeline, which is the only timeline that was ever going to work. If you catch yourself wanting more, write the urge down instead of acting on it, and notice, at the end of the week, how little of what you wanted to know you actually needed. That noticing is the lesson. The relationships that survive the disclosure question are almost never the ones where someone asked the perfect question at the perfect moment. They are the ones where a person made it safe to be known, and then had the patience to let being known happen slowly. And if it turns out you never learn the whole story, that is not a loss to mourn. A person you can be close to without possessing, whose history stays theirs even as your life grows into theirs, is a person you can actually love rather than merely know. Then, and only then, does the question of what happens in the first uncertain weeks, the texting and the silences and the ordinary vertigo of not knowing where you stand, become one you can actually handle. That is next.

Chapter 3: Reading Pace, Not Minds

I will confess something, because it makes the rest of this chapter truthful. For a stretch of my life I mistook speed for depth. If a new relationship escalated fast, if we were texting all day by the second week and calling each other the good words by the fourth, I read that as a sign we had something rare. It took me an embarrassingly long time, and more than one crash, to learn that fast is not the same as deep, and that in the early weeks of dating anyone, and especially someone with trauma, the speed of merging tells you almost nothing about the strength of what you are building. Sometimes it tells you the opposite.

The first weeks are their own distinct terrain, and they deserve their own chapter, because the mistakes people make here are quiet and feel like love while they are happening. This is the stretch where you decide, mostly without noticing you are deciding, how fast to weave your life into someone else's. Get the pace wrong here and everything downstream gets harder. Get it right and you give the relationship the one thing it actually needs to become real, which is time.

The pull to merge, and why it is strongest now

There is a gravity in early dating that pulls two people toward fast fusion. You start rearranging your week around them. Your friends hear the name constantly. You cancel the plans you would not have canceled a month ago. Your routines, your sleep, your moods begin to sync to theirs. It feels wonderful, because merging releases the very chemistry that makes early love intoxicating, and it feels like progress, like you are getting somewhere.

But merging fast is not the same as connecting deeply, and in a trauma-aware relationship the difference is sharp. For a partner whose nervous system is oriented toward threat, rapid closeness can be a lot, faster than their body can process as safe, even when they want it in their mind. And for you, fast merging quietly erases the vantage point you need most in the early weeks, which is enough separateness to actually see the relationship you are in. When you have fused with someone by week three, you have lost the ability to assess them, because assessing requires a little distance, and you gave the distance away.

Novaire, thirty-three, is the example I think about. He met someone early in the year and within a month they were, in his words, inseparable. Every evening together, constant contact through the day, plans already sketched for months ahead. He felt certain, and the certainty felt like the point. What he could not see, from inside the fusion, was that the certainty was doing his thinking for him. He had merged so completely and so fast that when small warning signs appeared, a flash of contempt here, a controlling comment there, he had no separate ground to stand on to evaluate them. He was already all in. It took a friend, gently, to ask him a question that landed like cold water: "You have known this person for six weeks. What do you actually know about how they treat you when things are hard?" He did not have an answer. He had a feeling, and he had mistaken the feeling for knowledge.

The Borrowed Certainty

That is the principle for this chapter. The Borrowed Certainty: in the early weeks, the confidence you feel about a relationship is usually borrowed against time you have not yet spent, and fast merging is how you take out that loan without noticing. Real certainty is earned slowly, by watching how someone behaves across many ordinary situations, especially the ones that go wrong. Early merging skips the earning and hands you the feeling of certainty for free, which is exactly why it is dangerous. You feel sure, and the sureness is not backed by anything yet.

The correction is not to be cold or to hold someone at arm's length as a strategy. It is to let the relationship move at the speed of actual knowledge. Stay a little bit yourself. Keep some of your evenings. Keep your friends close and your routines intact. Not as a test of the other person, but as a way of preserving the vantage point from which you can see clearly. If the relationship is good, this costs you nothing, because a good relationship does not require you to disappear into it by week three. If the relationship is not good, this separateness is the thing that will let you notice in time.

Contact frequency, and the rhythm conversation

One of the most concrete places the pace question shows up is contact. How much do you text? How often do you see each other? What does a normal week look like? In trauma-aware dating this can get tangled, because a partner who needs solitude to regulate might go quieter than you expect, and you can read the quiet as distance and respond by reaching harder, which creates exactly the pressure their system was trying to step away from.

The move here is not to guess and not to demand. It is to have what I call a rhythm conversation, early and lightly. You simply say something like, "I like talking to you and I do not want to assume the pace. What feels good to you, day to day, with texting and how often we see each other?" This does something a demand never could. It treats the pace as a thing you set together, out loud, rather than a thing you each privately expect and quietly resent when the other gets it wrong. It also gives your partner permission to tell you they sometimes need space, without that need being a rejection.

I want to be careful here, because there is a subtle trap. Partners of people with trauma sometimes slide into accommodation, quietly reshaping their own behavior around the other person's avoidance until the relationship organizes itself entirely around what the anxious or numb partner can tolerate. Researchers studying couples affected by trauma have found that this kind of accommodation, adjusting your life to help your partner avoid distress, is associated with lower relationship functioning over time, above and beyond either person's individual distress (Fredman et al., 2014). Accommodating a little, flexibly, is kindness. Rebuilding your whole life around someone else's comfort is the beginning of self-erasure, and it does not even help them. The rhythm conversation is the antidote, because it keeps the pace a negotiation between two people rather than a silent surrender by one.

When you are already organizing your life around them

Attachment research offers a useful lens here, and I will keep it light because you are not a case study either. People differ in how they handle closeness and distance. Some of us, when a relationship feels uncertain, get anxious and reach harder, wanting more contact, more reassurance, more merging, as a way to quiet the fear (Mikulincer & Shaver, 2016). Others pull back when things get close. Neither of these is a flaw, but knowing your own tendency changes what you do in the early weeks.

If you lean anxious, the early weeks with a trauma-affected partner can be genuinely hard, because their occasional need for space will press directly on your fear, and your instinct will be to close the gap fast. That instinct, followed, produces the fusion that costs you your vantage point. So the work, if this is you, is to notice the reach before you act on it, and to put the energy somewhere else, into your own friends, your own life, your own steadiness, rather than into your partner's inbox.

Auren, twenty-seven, recognized this pattern in herself only after it had cost her something. She had a habit, when a new partner went quiet, of filling the silence with her whole self, canceling plans to be available, checking her phone through dinner with friends, reorganizing her days around the possibility of contact. With a partner who needed regular solitude, this became a loop. He would step back to breathe. She would surge forward to reassure herself. He would feel crowded and step back further. She read the further step as proof she needed to try harder. The relationship did not survive it, and the plain lesson she took was not about him. It was that her own pace, her own steady separate life, was the thing she had abandoned first, before he ever gave her a reason to.

Auren's next relationship went differently, not because she found someone with less need for space, but because she kept herself this time. When her partner went quiet, she noticed the old reach, named it privately, and then went to her own life instead of his. The quiet passed, as quiet usually does. And because she had not merged herself out of existence, she could actually see, over the following months, that this person was kind and consistent, which was information she had never been able to gather before, because she had always been too fused to look.

Future talk before present knowledge

There is a specific flavor of fast merging that deserves its own warning, because it disguises itself so well as romance. It is future talk. The early conversations that leap ahead, where you are already discussing the trip you will take next summer, the city you might live in together, the shape of a life you have not begun to test. Future talk feels like commitment, and in a healthy relationship on a healthy timeline it eventually is. In the first few weeks it is something else. It is a way of manufacturing certainty about a person you do not yet know, by borrowing against a future you are imagining rather than a present you have observed.

With a partner who has trauma, rapid future talk carries an extra weight. It can raise the stakes faster than the relationship can bear, turning something that should feel light and exploratory into something loaded, where backing out or slowing down now feels like a betrayal of promises made too early. Notice when the conversation keeps drifting into the far future, and gently keep bringing it back to the present. Not by refusing to dream, but by staying clear that dreaming is not the same as knowing. You can enjoy someone's company enormously and still say, to yourself, I do not know yet whether this is a next-summer relationship, because I have not seen enough of who this person is when things are hard. Holding that clarity is not pessimism. It is the discipline that keeps you free.

Protecting the people who can see for you

When you merge fast, the first casualties are usually your friends, and that matters more than it seems, because your friends are the people who can see the relationship from the outside when you no longer can.

Novaire, remember, needed a friend to ask him the cold-water question, because he had lost his own ability to ask it. If he had let that friendship fade during the fusion, as people often do, there would have been no one positioned to say the thing he needed to hear.

So in the early weeks, treat your outside relationships as essential infrastructure, not as things to be set aside now that someone exciting has arrived. Keep the standing plans. Tell your close people what is happening and, more importantly, let them tell you what they see. This is not about assembling a jury to judge your partner. It is about keeping intact the network of perspective that fusion quietly dissolves. The people who love you and are not in love with your partner can often see, months before you can, whether you are being treated well. Do not cut yourself off from them at precisely the moment their sight is most valuable.

There is a version of this that trauma-aware daters get wrong out of loyalty. They feel that talking to friends about the relationship, especially about their partner's struggles, would be a violation of the partner's privacy, so they go silent, and the silence isolates them. There is a real line here, and you should not narrate your partner's trauma history to your friends as gossip. But you are allowed to have support. You are allowed to say, to someone you trust, I am finding this hard and I need to think out loud. Keeping your own support is not disloyalty. It is one of the things that will let you show up steadily for your partner instead of drowning quietly beside them.

The action: a pace inventory

Here is what to do this week. Take a candid inventory of how merged you already are, and do it in writing, because writing makes it harder to lie to yourself. Ask five questions. How many of my evenings this week were shaped around them? How many of my own plans have I dropped or delayed since we started? Do my friends feel further away than they did a month ago? When we are apart, is my attention actually free, or is it circling their next message? And, the important one: if I had to assess how this person treats me when things go wrong, could I, or have I not seen enough yet because it has all moved too fast?

You are not looking for a particular answer. You are looking at yourself. If the inventory shows you have merged fast, the correction is gentle and immediate. Reclaim an evening. Text a friend you have neglected. Let a silence be a silence instead of an emergency. You are not pulling away from your partner. You are stepping back onto the ground from which you can actually see them, which is the only ground from which love that lasts ever gets built. Do the inventory truthfully, and then do one small thing to reclaim a piece of your own life before the week is out, one evening, one friend, one hour of attention that is genuinely yours. That single act of stepping back is not a retreat from love. It is the beginning of the only kind of love that can survive being looked at clearly. Certainty, if it is going to come at all, will come from months of watching someone be themselves across ordinary days, not from weeks of feeling sure while you are too merged to look. Give it the months. The relationships worth having can survive being known slowly, and the ones that cannot survive it were telling you something you needed to hear before you handed them your whole life. Slow is not the same as uninterested. It is how careful people build the things that last. And once you can see them, the next question becomes bearable, the one about all those silences and slow replies, and the stories your mind writes to fill them.

Chapter 4: The Stories Silence Tells

Elorien was certain it was over. She was thirty, four months into a relationship that had been good, and her partner had not replied to her last two messages, sent the evening before and again that morning. By noon she had constructed the entire ending. He had lost interest. Something she said at dinner two nights ago had landed wrong. He was, at this very moment, drafting the kind message that ends things. She had read the whole breakup off the back of a silent phone, and she had done it so vividly that when he finally texted at three, a warm and ordinary message about a hard day at work and needing to go quiet for a bit, she felt almost disoriented, because the relationship in her head had already died and here it was, alive, asking if she wanted to get dinner Thursday.

Nothing had happened except silence. Everything else, the whole catastrophe, she had written herself. This chapter is about that writing, because the space between messages is where trauma-aware dating quietly breaks people, and the thing that breaks them is not usually the silence. It is the story they tell about the silence.

Silence is data, not a verdict

Start with a distinction that will save you more grief than almost anything else in this book. A silence is a fact. It is data. Your partner has not replied. That is all you actually know. Everything past that, the interpretation, the meaning, the story about what it says about you and them and the future, is something you are adding, and you are usually adding it without evidence, in the worst possible mood, at the worst possible speed.

This matters especially with a partner who has trauma, because their silences will be more frequent and less legible than you might expect from someone else. A lasting sense of current threat, one of the defining features of post-traumatic stress, does not switch off because a relationship is going well (van der Kolk, 2014). Sometimes your partner will go quiet because they are overwhelmed, or regulating, or simply need solitude to come back to themselves, and none of it will be about you. The National Center for PTSD notes plainly that withdrawal and numbing in a partner with trauma can make them feel present but emotionally absent, and that this is a feature of the condition rather than a message about the relationship (National Center for PTSD, n.d.). The silence is often not even addressed to you. You just happen to be standing where it lands.

The Narrator Trap

Here is the principle, and I want you to feel how much rides on it. The Narrator Trap: when someone goes quiet, your mind rushes in to narrate the silence, and because the narration feels like thinking, you mistake the story for the truth. The trap is not the silence. The trap is believing the narrator. Your mind, faced with ambiguity, does not sit calmly with not knowing. It generates an explanation, and it hands you that explanation with a false certainty, and the explanation it generates when you are anxious is almost always about threat, loss, and your own fault.

The narrator is not lying to hurt you. It is doing what minds do, which is to resolve uncertainty as fast as possible, because uncertainty feels dangerous. But a fast answer is not a true answer, and the stories the narrator tells during a silence have a very poor track record. Elorien's narrator had told her the same story in three previous relationships. It had been wrong all three times. And still, in the fourth, it spoke with total confidence, because that is what the narrator does. It does not learn. It just narrates.

Once you can see the narrator as a narrator, something shifts. You stop asking is this story true and start asking a better question: is this something I know, or something I am telling myself? Almost always, during a silence, the frightening version is the telling, not the knowing. You do not know he is losing interest. You know he has not texted back. Those are not the same, and the whole art of surviving the silences is refusing to let the second quietly become the first.

The practice: wait, do not narrate

Knowing about the narrator is not enough, because the narrator is faster than your knowledge. You need a practice, something to do with your body and your attention while the story is trying to write itself. I call it, plainly, wait, do not narrate.

When you notice the silence and feel the narration starting, the pull to explain, to decode, to figure out what it means, you do three things. First, you name it to yourself, silently and without drama: the narrator is going. Just naming it creates a sliver of distance between you and the story. Second, you refuse to act on the story. You do not send the anxious follow-up, the double text, the casual message that is actually a check for reassurance. The narration will demand action, because acting feels like relief, but the action almost always makes things worse, adding pressure to a partner who went quiet precisely because they needed less. Third, you move your attention, deliberately, onto your own life. Not as a trick to make them text back, but because your attention is yours and it does not have to sit vigil by a phone. Go do the thing you would do if you were not waiting. Let the silence be a silence while you live inside your own afternoon.

This is hard, and it is harder if you lean anxious, and it does not get easy the first time. But it gets easier every time you do it and discover, again, that the silence meant something ordinary, that the catastrophe your narrator promised did not arrive. You are teaching your nervous system a new association: silence, then nothing terrible, then an ordinary explanation. Do it enough and the narrator gets quieter, not because you argued it into submission, but because you stopped rewarding it with your obedience.

Asking for a rhythm you can both live with

Waiting well is half of it. The other half is that you are allowed to want a communication rhythm that works for you, and you are allowed to ask for it. Enduring silences with grace does not mean pretending you have no needs. It means addressing your needs through open conversation rather than through anxious reaching.

The move is the rhythm conversation from the last chapter, applied to silence specifically. At a calm moment, not in the middle of a quiet spell and not laced with accusation, you say something like: "When you go quiet for a while, I sometimes start imagining the worst, and I would rather not do that. Would it work for you to send even a short note, just so I know it is you needing space and not something wrong between us?" Notice what this does. It does not demand constant contact, which a trauma-affected partner may genuinely be unable to give. It asks for one small, specific thing, a signal, a word, that lets you tell the difference between regulation and rupture. Many partners can offer that even when they cannot offer more, and having it changes everything, because it takes the ambiguity out of the silence, and ambiguity is what the narrator feeds on.

If your partner cannot or will not offer even that, over time, that is itself information, and we will come back to it in later chapters. But start by asking, kindly and specifically, because a great deal of the pain of silence dissolves the moment there is an agreed signal that says this quiet is normal, I am okay, we are okay.

The myth that caring means always replying

There is a belief hiding under most silence-panic, and it is worth dragging into the light. The belief is that if someone cares about you, they will always reply promptly, and therefore a delay must mean diminished care. Held up to daylight, this falls apart immediately. You have gone quiet on people you love. You have needed a day. You have been underwater at work, or flattened by your own mood, or simply out of words, and none of it meant you had stopped caring. You know this about yourself and forget it instantly about your partner the moment the phone goes quiet.

With a trauma-affected partner, the belief is not just wrong, it is actively harmful, because the very thing that helps them, occasional space to regulate, gets recoded by your narrator as evidence of fading love. If you hold someone to a standard of constant responsiveness, you punish them for the exact self-care that keeps them steady. Retire the belief. Replace it with a truer one: care is shown across time, in how someone treats you when they are present, not in the speed of every reply. A partner who is warm, open, and reconnecting when they return is showing care, even if their texting rhythm will never match yours.

Your own body in the waiting

The silence does something to your body, and pretending otherwise does not help. Your chest tightens, your attention narrows to the phone, a low alarm hums under everything you try to do. This is real, and it is not a character flaw. It is your own system responding to uncertainty. The mistake is trying to end the discomfort by ending the uncertainty, which is what reaching for the phone is really about. You are not trying to reach them. You are trying to make the feeling stop.

So tend to the feeling directly, on its own terms, without routing it through your partner. Move your body, because movement metabolizes anxiety in a way that thinking never will. Put your attention on something that requires it, work, a friend, a task, anything that gives your mind a job other than narrating. Let the discomfort be present without treating it as an emergency that must be resolved this instant. The discomfort will pass on its own, usually faster than you expect, and it will pass whether or not your partner texts, which is the whole point. Your peace during a silence cannot be outsourced to another person's phone. It has to be something you can generate yourself, and learning to generate it is one of the quiet superpowers of trauma-aware dating, because it frees you from needing your partner to manage your anxiety for you. That freedom is a gift to both of you.

When quiet is regulation, and when it is avoidance

Not all silence is the same, and part of reading pace instead of minds is learning, over time, to tell two kinds apart. There is quiet that is regulation, a temporary stepping back to come back to oneself, and there is quiet that is avoidance, a pattern of disappearing from anything difficult rather than facing it. Regulation tends to return. The person goes quiet, and then they come back, and the coming back includes some acknowledgment, some repair, some sense that you were held in mind even during the silence. Avoidance tends to leave things unaddressed, to let hard conversations evaporate into quiet and never resurface, so that nothing ever gets worked through.

You cannot tell these apart from a single silence, and you should not try, because a single silence is just data. You tell them apart across time, by watching the pattern. Does the quiet resolve, or does it swallow every difficult thing whole? Does your partner come back and reconnect, or does the silence become the way problems get disappeared? This is not about diagnosing anyone. It is about noticing, patiently, whether the rhythm between you includes return and repair, or whether it includes only vanishing. Avoidance and emotional numbing are among the trauma responses most associated with relationship strain, precisely because they pull a person away from the repair that relationships run on (Campbell & Renshaw, 2012; Fredman et al., 2014). But whether a given pattern is workable is a question for later chapters. For now, the skill is simply to watch across time instead of reacting to each silence as if it were the whole story.

Cyrel, thirty-six, learned this slowly and with a lot of self-correction. His partner went quiet in ways that frightened him early on, and his narrator was loud. What helped was not becoming numb to the silences but getting curious about the pattern over months. He noticed, eventually, that her quiet almost always resolved, that she came back, that she named it, that the silences were regulation and not abandonment. That noticing let him relax into the rhythm rather than fight it. It is worth saying that it does not always resolve this way. For some couples the watching reveals avoidance that never repairs, and that is a harder story with a different ending. Cyrel's revealed regulation, and he was able to trust it because he had actually watched, over time, rather than deciding after the first quiet week.

The action: one silence, narrated and un-narrated

Here is your work this week. The next time your partner goes quiet and you feel the narrator start, catch it, and do the practice. Name the narrator. Refuse the anxious action. Move your attention to your own life. And then, when the silence eventually breaks, as it almost always does, do one more thing: compare. Compare the story your narrator told you to what actually turned out to be true. Write both down if it helps. Over a few rounds of this, you will build a private record of how often the narrator was wrong, and that record is the thing that finally loosens its grip. You cannot argue yourself out of the Narrator Trap in the moment. But you can, over time, stop believing a narrator with a documented history of being wrong. The narrator will not disappear entirely, and it does not have to. You are not trying to become someone who feels nothing when a message goes unanswered, which is neither possible nor desirable. You are trying to become someone who can feel the pull of the story and decline to believe it, who can let a silence stay a silence long enough for the truth to arrive on its own. That skill, practiced across enough silences, is the difference between a relationship you get to experience and a relationship you merely survive. You get better at this every time you let a silence pass without a catastrophe arriving to prove you right. That is the whole move. Silence stays silence. The story stays a story. And you stay steady in the space between, which is exactly where the next challenge lives, because sometimes the distance comes not before closeness but right after it, and that particular pattern deserves a chapter of its own.

Chapter 5: When Closeness Brings Distance

Here is a claim that sounds wrong until you have lived it: sometimes the better the night goes, the more likely your partner is to disappear the next day. Not despite the closeness. Because of it. Sevrin found this out the hard way, and spent weeks looking for the mistake he must have made, before he understood there had been no mistake at all.

Sevrin, thirty-two, had been seeing someone for a couple of months, and one evening everything aligned. A long dinner, real laughter, a conversation that went deeper than either had gone before, a night that ended close. He woke up happy. By afternoon she had gone quiet, and by the next day she was distant in a way that frightened him, formal almost, as if the evening had never happened. His mind did exactly what you would expect. It searched the night for the moment he had ruined it. Had he said too much? Wanted too much? Been too much? He found a dozen candidate crimes and confessed to all of them in an anxious message that only made things worse. What he did not yet understand was that the closeness itself was the thing his partner's system had reacted to, and that his frantic pursuit was pressing on exactly the place that needed room.

Why good nights can trip an alarm

For a nervous system shaped by trauma, closeness is not a simple good. It can be wonderful and it can be a signal of exposure at the same time, because closeness means lowered defenses, and lowered defenses is precisely the state that once, in the past, preceded harm. The body does not file this distinction carefully. It notices that it has opened, feels the vulnerability of being open, and pulls back to restore a sense of safety. The pulling back is not a verdict on you or on the evening. It is a reflex older than the relationship, doing the only job it knows.

There is research that speaks directly to this, and it is worth knowing because it moves the whole thing out of the category of personal failure. In a study of couples having supportive, warm conversations, the exact kind of moment that should feel purely good, higher post-traumatic stress symptoms were linked to more fear and negative emotion when a partner offered caring, validation, and understanding, not less (Leifker et al., 2015). Read that again. The intimacy did not soothe the reactivity. It stirred it. The pleasant moment and the internal alarm were happening in the same body at the same time. So when your partner is warm and open one night and withdrawn the next, you are not watching a person who changed their mind. You are watching a person whose system is metabolizing an experience that was good and destabilizing at once.

The National Center for PTSD describes this pattern in plainer terms, noting that a partner with trauma can seem present and then emotionally absent, and that the numbing and distancing are features of the condition rather than a message about the relationship (National Center for PTSD, n.d.). None of this requires you to diagnose anyone or to become an expert in their inner workings. It requires one shift: to stop reading the distance as caused by you, and to start reading it as a wave that rose because the water got deep.

The Alarm of Closeness

Name it so you can hold it. The Alarm of Closeness: for some trauma survivors, intimacy itself can set off an internal alarm, so that a period of real closeness is followed by a period of distance, not because anything went wrong, but because something went right and the system needs to recover from how exposed that felt. The closer you got, the louder the alarm, the greater the pullback. It is a rhythm, not a rupture.

Once you can see it as a rhythm, your job changes completely. When you read the distance as evidence of a mistake, your instinct is to pursue, to fix, to close the gap and get reassurance that everything is fine. That instinct, followed, is the worst possible move, because it adds pressure to a system that withdrew in order to find room. You chase, they retreat further, you read the further retreat as confirmation of disaster, and the loop tightens. When you read the distance as an alarm that will quiet on its own, your instinct is different. You give room. You stay warm but unhurried. You let the wave crest and fall without treating it as an emergency, and you trust, from experience, that the closeness returns once the system feels safe again.

What to do while they are far

Giving room is not the same as going cold, and this is the part people get wrong. Withdrawing your warmth in retaliation, going distant to match their distance, teaches your partner that closeness is genuinely dangerous, that opening up gets punished with abandonment. That is the opposite of what you want. What you want is to be the steady thing that does not vanish, the fixed point they can drift from and return to without losing.

So while they are far, do three things. Stay warm without demanding a response. A light, no-pressure message that expects nothing back, something that communicates I am here and I am not upset, is very different from an anxious bid for reassurance. Keep living your own life, fully, so that your steadiness is real and not a performance, and so that your peace does not depend on their return. And hold the knowledge, from the pattern you have watched, that this is a wave and not the end. If you have seen the closeness return before, let that memory steady you now.

Sevrin learned this on the second and third rounds, not the first. The first time, he chased, and it went badly. The second time, he made himself wait, and it was agonizing, and it worked. She came back within a few days, and when she did, she said something that reorganized his understanding. She said the night had been the best in a long time, and that was exactly why she had needed to disappear for a bit, because good scared her more than bad did. He had spent the whole distance believing he had failed at closeness. She had needed the distance because the closeness had succeeded.

The rhythm conversation, applied to distance

You do not have to be a silent, patient monk about this forever. At a calm moment, when you are close and not in the middle of a pullback, you can name the pattern gently and ask about it. Something like: "I have noticed that after we have a really good, close time, you sometimes need some distance afterward. I think I understand it a little, and I want you to know you can take that space without me falling apart. Is there anything that would make those stretches easier for both of us?"

This does several things at once. It shows your partner you see the pattern without pathologizing it. It gives them permission to take space without guilt, which reduces the shame that often makes the withdrawal worse. And it opens the door to small agreements, a signal, a word, a check-in, that make the distance less frightening for you. Many partners, asked kindly, can offer something. Even a text that just says wave, meaning I am in the pullback and I am okay and I will be back, can transform the experience for both of you.

The myth that closeness should always feel simple

Underneath the panic when your partner withdraws is usually a belief you absorbed from every love story you have ever seen: that if someone really wants you, closeness will feel easy for them, and any complication around it means the wanting is not real. It is a lovely belief and it is false for almost everyone, and it is especially false here. Wanting closeness and being destabilized by closeness are not opposites. They live in the same person, often in the same hour. Your partner can want you badly and still need to step back from how much they want you, because the wanting itself is the exposure their system learned to fear.

If you hold your partner to the myth, you will misread every pullback as a failure of desire, and you will keep asking, in a hundred anxious ways, do you still want me, which is the one question that makes the alarm louder. Trade the myth for something truer. Closeness, for a trauma survivor, can be a place of both longing and threat, and a partner who withdraws after intimacy is often not wanting you less but feeling you more than their system knows how to hold. That reframe will not make the distance comfortable. It will make it survivable, and it will stop you from adding your fear to theirs.

Building a way back in

The most useful thing a couple can do about this pattern is not to prevent the waves, which cannot be prevented, but to build a reliable way back together after them. Left unspoken, the return is awkward. The distance breaks, and neither of you knows how to bridge from cold back to warm, so you both pretend nothing happened, which leaves the pattern unaddressed and a little heavier each time. Named and agreed on in advance, the return becomes something you do on purpose.

This can be simple. Some couples agree on a small signal that means the wave has passed and I am ready to come back, a phrase, a gesture, a particular kind of message. Some agree that when the closeness returns, they will name the wave out loud, briefly and without blame, so it stops being a secret. That was a hard few days, I missed you, I am glad you are back. The point is not to analyze the withdrawal to death. It is to give the reconnection a shape, so that opening back up does not require either of you to be brave from scratch every single time. When the way back is known, the distance loses some of its menace, because both of you can see the far shore even while you are apart.

There is a version of this that asks something of you specifically. When your partner returns, resist the urge to relitigate the distance, to make them explain and account for every hour they were gone, to extract an apology for a reflex. That turns the return into a trial, and it teaches them that coming back is dangerous, which makes them slower to come back next time. Meet the return with warmth, not with an invoice. You can talk about the pattern later, at a calm moment, as its own conversation. In the moment of reconnection, the kindest and most strategic thing you can do is simply be glad they are here.

Where patience ends

This book will keep drawing this line because it matters more than any single technique. Understanding the Alarm of Closeness does not obligate you to tolerate any amount of distance for any length of time forever. There is a difference between a wave that rises and falls, closeness followed by distance followed by return and reconnection, and a pattern where the distance never resolves, where every time you get close your partner disappears and does not come back, or comes back without any acknowledgment, or uses the withdrawal as a way to avoid every hard thing indefinitely. The first is a rhythm you can work with. The second is a wall, and no amount of patience turns a wall into a door.

Maevren, twenty-nine, had to face this distinction squarely. She had read every gentle book, learned to give space beautifully, and given it, and given it, for the better part of a year. But the closeness never returned in any lasting way. Every time she and her partner got near something real, he vanished, and the vanishing never came back around to repair. She kept telling herself it was the Alarm of Closeness and she just needed more patience. What she finally admitted was that a rhythm returns and this never returned, that she had been calling a wall a wave because the wave was the version she could bear. She left, and grieved, and was right to. Her patience had not been the problem. Her patience had been genuine and generous. The relationship had simply asked her to accept permanent distance and call it love, and she had finally declined.

What a no-pressure message actually sounds like

People hear stay warm without demanding a response and freeze, because the line between warm and needy can feel invisible in the moment. Here is the test. A warm message gives something and asks for nothing. A needy message looks like giving but is actually asking, usually asking for reassurance. Saw this and thought of you, no reply needed, hope your week is gentle is warm. Are we okay? You have been quiet and I am worried, did I do something? is a bid dressed as concern, and your partner will feel the difference instantly. One lets them rest in the distance knowing you are steady. The other hands them a job to do, your reassurance, at exactly the moment they have the least to give.

If you cannot tell which one you are about to send, wait. Sit with the discomfort a little longer and send it later, or do not send it at all. Nothing bad happens in the silence that your anxious message would prevent, and quite a lot of good happens in a partner learning that they can go quiet and you will neither vanish nor pursue. That steadiness is a rare thing to offer someone whose history taught them that closeness always comes with a catch. Being the person without a catch is most of the work.

The action: name one wave

Here is your work this week, and it is an observation, not a confrontation. If you are in the middle of a pullback, do not chase. Instead, notice it as a wave. Write down, privately, three things: when the distance started, what happened right before it, whether the thing right before it was actually closeness rather than conflict, and what you are afraid it means. Then set the note aside and give room. When the closeness returns, and if the pattern is a rhythm rather than a wall it usually will, come back to the note and see what was true. You are building the same kind of record you built with the narrator, a private history of what the distance actually meant, so that next time your fear has something real to argue against. And you are learning, wave by wave, to tell the rhythm you can live with from the wall you cannot, which is the quiet, unglamorous skill that this whole book is really about.

Chapter 6: Touch, Sex, and Ongoing Yes

Most of us were taught to think of consent as a gate. You ask once, you get a yes, and then you are through, and the yes covers everything that follows. That model is not just thin, it is actively unsafe when you are building intimacy with a trauma survivor, and this chapter asks you to trade it for something better. Consent is not a gate you pass through once. It is a conversation that stays open the whole time, and either of you can change the answer at any moment without owing anyone an explanation.

A brief, candid note before we go further. Physical intimacy after trauma is deep water, and this chapter offers a way of thinking, not a clinical protocol. If either of you is working through significant trauma around touch or sex, the best version of this includes support from a therapist or a consent educator who knows your actual situation. What follows is the relational foundation the rest rests on. It is not a substitute for that care.

Why the gate model fails

The gate model assumes a stable self behind the yes, a person whose desire, once expressed, stays put. Trauma complicates that assumption in ways worth understanding without pathologizing. Trauma lives in the body, not just the memory, and touch can call it up faster than thought, so a person can be fully willing one moment and, without warning to themselves, find their body somewhere else the next (van der Kolk, 2014). Something that felt good on Tuesday can feel like too much on Friday, or feel like too much halfway through the same encounter, not because your partner is being difficult but because their nervous system is doing something older and faster than choice.

If you are holding the gate model, this reads as rejection or as mixed signals, and you respond with hurt or with pressure, both of which make the body less safe, not more. If you are holding the open-conversation model, the same moment reads as information. Something shifted. We can slow down or stop. That reframe is the whole difference between intimacy that heals and intimacy that re-wounds. Herman, in her foundational work on trauma recovery, put safety first among the stages of healing, before anything else becomes possible (Herman, 1992). In a relationship, safety is not a mood you create once. It is a practice you renew, and consent that stays open is what the practice looks like in the body.

The Living Yes

Here is the principle. The Living Yes: real consent is alive, which means it can change, and a yes that cannot become a no at any moment was never a full yes to begin with. The goal is not to collect a yes and keep it. The goal is to build the kind of closeness where a no is completely safe to say, because only when no is safe does yes mean anything.

Notice how much this asks of you, and how much it gives back. It asks you to hold your own desire loosely enough that you can set it down the instant your partner's answer changes, without sulking, without making them manage your disappointment, without any cost to them for stopping. That is a real discipline, and it is not always easy. What it gives back is enormous. A partner who knows, in their body, that you will stop the moment they need to, that stopping costs them nothing, that their no is met with care rather than injury, is a partner who can actually relax into a yes. The freedom to stop is what makes it safe to start. Couples who chase the yes and treat the no as failure end up with less intimacy, not more, because the body cannot open where it is not free to close.

How checking in becomes natural

The fear people have is that all this checking in will kill the mood, turn intimacy into a clumsy series of consent forms. It does the opposite, once you learn to do it as connection rather than interruption. Checking in is not a legal procedure. It is attention. It sounds like is this good, it sounds like slower, it sounds like a pause to read your partner's face and body and actually see them. Done well, it is not a break from intimacy. It is intimacy, because being genuinely watched and responded to is one of the most connecting experiences there is.

The tone matters more than the words. Checking in from anxiety, are you sure this is okay, are you okay, did I do something, puts the burden on your partner to reassure you, which is its own kind of pressure. Checking in from warmth, tell me what feels good, we can go as slow as you want, I love just being close like this, invites rather than interrogates. You are not asking your partner to certify your performance. You are telling them, through your attention, that their experience is the thing you are tracking, and that there is no wrong answer, including stop.

Solenne, thirty-four, and her partner Zevian, thirty-six, built this slowly and not without awkwardness. Early on, Solenne would freeze mid-closeness sometimes, go somewhere far in her eyes, and the first few times it happened Zevian took it personally and got quiet and wounded, which made Solenne feel she had failed him on top of everything else. What changed things was a conversation with the lights on and their clothes on, where they agreed on something simple: that either of them could stop anything at any time by just saying pause, and that pause would always be met with okay and never with a why. The first time Solenne used it, Zevian said okay, and meant it, and held her, and asked for nothing. She cried, a little, from relief. It was the first time stopping had ever been safe. Their intimacy did not shrink after that. It deepened, because it finally had somewhere safe to grow.

When something shifts mid-closeness

You will not always get a clear pause. Sometimes your partner will go distant, or tense, or absent, without a word, and you will have to notice it yourself. This is where attention earns its keep. If you feel your partner leave, in their body or their eyes, the move is to slow down and gently offer an exit, not to push through and not to demand an explanation. Something like, let us slow down, or we can just be close like this, or there is no rush and nothing has to happen. You are handing them the off-ramp without making them ask for it, which for someone who learned that their no did not matter is a profound thing to receive.

What you do not do is interrogate the shift in the moment. Now is not the time for what happened, are you okay, did I trigger something. Those questions, however loving, ask your partner to process and explain at exactly the moment they have the least capacity for it, and they center your need to understand over their need for safety. Understanding can come later, at a calm time, if they want to share it. In the moment, the whole job is to make the exit easy and the landing soft. You can talk tomorrow. Tonight, just be the person who noticed and slowed down and asked for nothing.

The myth that talking about it ruins it

The belief that keeps couples stuck here is that good intimacy is spontaneous and wordless, that if you have to talk about it you have already lost the magic. This is one of the most expensive myths in dating, and it is worth naming plainly. The wordless, mind-reading intimacy that the movies sell does not exist, and chasing it with a trauma survivor is a way of guaranteeing that neither of you ever feels safe. What the myth calls magic is usually just two people who got lucky and did not have to negotiate. What actually produces reliable, deepening intimacy over time is the opposite of mind-reading. It is the freedom to say what is true.

Trade the myth for a better standard. The couples with the best intimacy are not the ones who never speak. They are the ones for whom speaking is safe, who can say slower or not tonight or I loved that without it becoming a crisis. Words do not kill desire. Unspoken pressure kills desire, because a body cannot fully open while it is bracing for a no it is not allowed to say. Every truthful sentence you make safe between you is not a subtraction from the intimacy. It is the thing the intimacy is built out of. When your partner learns that talking is welcome, they stop having to choose between candor and closeness, and that is when closeness actually becomes possible.

Touch that is not going anywhere

For many trauma survivors, one of the most healing things a relationship can offer is touch that has no destination, closeness that is not a prelude to anything, contact that is not a request. When every touch is the opening move of a negotiation toward sex, the body stays a little braced even in the tender moments, because it is always half-anticipating the next step. Building in touch that is explicitly going nowhere, holding, resting together, a hand held with no agenda, gives the nervous system something rare: closeness it does not have to manage.

You can name this and offer it on purpose. Let us just be close, nothing has to happen, I like this exactly as it is. Said and meant, and then actually honored, this teaches your partner's body that being near you is not a slippery slope, that they can accept your touch without having consented to a whole evening's trajectory. Over time, that safety does something quietly powerful. It lets desire arise on its own, from a rested place, rather than being summoned under low-grade pressure. Couples who master non-goal-oriented touch often find that the goal-oriented kind gets easier, not harder, because the body has finally learned that closeness with you is safe by default.

There is a discipline in this for you, the same one running through the whole chapter. You have to be able to offer that touch and mean the nothing has to happen, even on the nights you were hoping something would. If your no-agenda touch is secretly an agenda, your partner will feel it, and the safety evaporates. The gift only works if it is real. Give the closeness freely, wanting nothing back, and you will often find you receive more than you would have by asking, not as a trick, but as a natural consequence of a body that finally got to rest.

Your own desire, and its limits

This chapter has asked a lot of you, and it would be misleading to pretend it costs nothing. Holding your desire loosely, being ready to stop, not taking a mid-closeness withdrawal personally, all of it is real work, and you are allowed to have needs of your own inside it. Trauma-aware intimacy is not a monastery where your wants disappear. You are allowed to want closeness, to want sex, to want to be desired. The Living Yes runs in both directions, which means your no is also always safe, and your yes also matters.

The place this gets hard is when your genuine needs and your partner's genuine limits do not currently line up, when you want a kind of closeness their system cannot safely offer right now. This is not a failure and it is not necessarily permanent, but it is real, and pretending otherwise helps no one. The candid move is to name it kindly, without pressure and without martyrdom, as a fact about where the two of you are rather than a verdict on either of you. I want you to know this is something I want, and I also completely understand it may not be where you are, and I am not asking you to be anywhere but where you are. Whether that gap is workable over time is a real question, and it belongs in the larger question this book keeps circling, of whether this relationship, as it actually is, fits the life you actually want. For now, the skill is to hold your own desire and your partner's safety in the same two hands, honoring both, sacrificing neither by default.

Afterward matters as much as during

Intimacy does not end when the physical part does. For a trauma survivor, the minutes after closeness can carry their own vulnerability, a strange exposure that arrives once the intensity fades, and how you handle those minutes teaches your partner whether opening up with you is safe to do again. A partner who withdraws immediately afterward, reaches for a phone, goes cold or distracted, can leave the other feeling used in a way that no amount of care during the act repairs. The afterward is where trust is either sealed or quietly broken.

You do not need a ritual, though some couples like one. You need presence. Stay. Be warm. Let there be a little softness on the other side of closeness, so that the whole experience, from the first touch to the settling quiet, tells your partner the same true thing: you are safe here, you were not just wanted for one moment, you are still here and so am

I. If your partner needs space afterward instead, that is theirs to have, and giving it warmly is its own kind of presence. The point is not a particular script. The point is that closeness lands somewhere gentle, so that the body files this encounter, start to finish, under safe.

The action: agree on a pause

Here is your work, and it is a conversation to have with the lights on, fully clothed, at a calm moment, not in bed and not in the middle of anything. Agree, out loud, on a way for either of you to stop or slow down anything physical, a single word or signal, and agree on what happens when it is used, which is that it is met with okay and care, every time, no questions, no wound, no cost. Practice saying it once to each other, awkwardly, so it exists before you need it. That one small agreement does more for intimacy than any technique, because it builds the floor of safety that everything else stands on. You are not making sex into paperwork. You are making stopping safe, which is the only thing that ever makes starting free. A yes that costs nothing to refuse is the only kind worth having, and building the safety that makes refusal costless is the work of many nights, not one. And a yes given freely, by a person who knows their no will be honored, is worth more than any yes you could have collected at a gate.

Chapter 7: When Something Gets Triggered

They were at a restaurant, a good one, celebrating nothing in particular, when a tray dropped somewhere behind them and shattered, and Orlian watched his date go from present and laughing to gone in the space of a breath. Her face changed. Her eyes went somewhere else. Her hands gripped the edge of the table. And Orlian, who liked this person more than he had liked anyone in a while, felt his own heart start to pound, because he had no idea what to do and every instinct he had was wrong.

This chapter is about that moment, the one where something gets triggered right in front of you, and it is the chapter people most want a script for. I will give you one, but first I have to take something away from you, because the thing you most want to do in that moment is the thing that helps least. You want to fix it. You want to say the perfect words that bring them back, to solve the trigger, to make the pain stop. You cannot, and trying is how you make it worse. What you can do is smaller, harder, and far more useful.

You cannot stop it, so stop trying to

Start with the hard truth, because everything good follows from accepting it. When your partner is triggered, their nervous system has responded to something as if it were a present threat, and that response is faster and older than your words. You cannot talk them out of it. You cannot love them out of it. You cannot find the magic sentence, because there is no magic sentence, and searching for one keeps you focused on your performance instead of on them. A trigger is the body reliving something, and the body does not take suggestions from the outside on demand (van der Kolk, 2014).

This is genuinely freeing once you accept it. You are not responsible for ending the trigger, because ending it is not in your power. You are responsible for one thing only: being a safe, steady presence while it passes. That is a job you can actually do. The National Center for PTSD, in its guidance for families, keeps returning to this same modest role, be calm, be safe, do not take it personally, rather than to any heroic intervention (National Center for PTSD, n.d.). Your calm is the offering. Not your wisdom, not your fix. Your calm.

Regulate yourself first

Here is the part that feels backward. The most helpful thing you can do for a triggered partner is to manage your own reaction first, because a triggered nervous system reads the room, and if your system is spiking too, theirs has one more threat to track. Orlian's pounding heart was not a private event. Had he let it drive him into panic, into a flurry of frantic questions and grabbing hands, he would have added his alarm to hers. The steadiest thing in the room becomes the thing a dysregulated system can borrow from, and you cannot be steady for someone else while you are drowning in your own fear.

So before you do anything for your partner, do one thing for yourself. Slow your own breathing. Drop your shoulders. Remind yourself, silently, this is not an emergency I have to solve, it is a wave I have to be steady through. This is not selfishness or detachment. It is the opposite. Your regulated presence is the actual help, and you cannot offer what you do not have. Put your own oxygen mask on, not because you matter more, but because a calm partner is worth more to a triggered person than a panicked one, every single time.

The Four-Step Pause

Now the sequence. Name it so you can find it under stress. The Four-Step Pause: notice, steady yourself, offer without imposing, and stay. Four moves, in order, none of them heroic, all of them within your power.

Notice. Register that something has shifted, and drop everything else. This is not the time to finish your story, press your point, or pretend it is not happening. The moment your partner goes somewhere else, your only agenda is this.

Steady yourself. Before you reach for them, get your own system under control, as we just covered. One slow breath. The reminder that this will pass and your job is presence, not rescue.

Offer without imposing. This is the delicate one. You do not grab, corner, or flood them with questions. You offer, gently and with options, and you let them choose. Would some quiet help? Do you want to step outside? Would you rather I am close or give you a little room? Offering with choice matters enormously, because a trigger is often a re-experiencing of powerlessness, and handing your partner control, even over something small, is the opposite of what the original harm did. If they cannot answer, that is fine. You simply lower the stimulation, get quieter, and wait.

Stay. You do not leave, and you do not make them perform being okay for your comfort. You remain a calm, available presence, near but not crowding, patient, unhurried, communicating through your steadiness that they are not too much and you are not going anywhere. The trigger will pass, as triggers do. Your job is to still be there, steady, when it does.

Aeris, thirty, learned the Four-Step Pause across several hard moments with a partner, and got it wrong before she got it right. Early on, when her partner froze, she flooded him, are you okay, what happened, what can I do, talk to me, a torrent of loving panic that gave his overwhelmed system a dozen more things to process. She could see it landing badly and could not stop herself, because her own fear was driving. What changed was learning to steady herself first. The next time, she caught her own spiral, took a breath, got quiet, and said only, I am right here, take your time. He came back faster than he ever had, and told her later that the quiet and the I am right here had been exactly what he could hold, when the torrent had been more than he could.

Afterward, do not interrogate

When your partner comes back, the trigger passed, you will be full of questions, and most of them you should not ask, at least not then. What was that, what happened to you, was it the sound, what does it mean, are these frequent. These questions serve your need to understand, and they arrive at the moment your partner has the least capacity to explain and the most vulnerability about having been seen in that state. Interrogating the trigger afterward can shame a person for a response they did not choose.

Instead, reconnect first, gently and without demand. I am glad you are back. That looked hard. You do not have to explain anything. Let them lead. If they want to tell you what happened, they will, in their own time, and your job is to receive it without turning it into a case study. If they do not want to talk about it, that is completely their right, and pressing for the story communicates that their trigger was an inconvenience you need explained. There may be a place, at a calm time later, for a larger conversation about what helps in those moments, and that conversation is genuinely useful. But it is a separate event from the trigger itself, and it happens on their terms, not in the raw minutes after.

When the trigger seems to involve you

Sometimes the trigger is a dropped tray, something external and obviously unrelated to you. Other times it is not so clean. Something you said, a tone you used, a move you made, a moment of conflict between you, and suddenly your partner is triggered, and now it feels personal, because in some sense it involved you. This is harder to hold, and it deserves its own treatment, because your instinct here is to get defensive, and defensiveness is the one thing that will make it worse.

Hold two things at once. It is possible that something you did touched an old wound, and it is also true that touching an old wound is not the same as having done something wrong. A raised voice, a sudden movement, a particular phrase can reach a place in your partner that has nothing to do with your intent and everything to do with their history. In that moment, the Four-Step Pause still applies. You still steady yourself, still offer without imposing, still stay. What you do not do is defend yourself, argue that you did nothing wrong, or demand that your partner see your good intentions right now. Your case, however valid, can wait. A triggered person cannot litigate fairness, and pressing them to is cruelty dressed as reason.

Later, when they are back and calm, there may be a real conversation to have, and it can hold both truths. You can learn that a certain tone lands hard for them, and adjust out of care, without accepting that you are a villain for having used it. And if the thing that triggered them was actually a legitimate problem with your behavior, later is when you own it. But in the moment, the trigger is not the trial. Steady first. Sort out fairness when the storm has passed, if there is anything left to sort.

When it happens in public

The restaurant, the party, the crowded street. Public triggers carry an extra layer, because now there is an audience, and your partner may feel not only the original overwhelm but the shame of being seen in it. Your job gains one quiet task: to lower the exposure without making a scene of lowering it. That can mean simply shifting your body to give them some visual privacy, suggesting stepping outside if they want it, or quietly handling the logistics, the check, the coats, the exit, so they do not have to perform competence while they are underwater.

The thing to avoid is turning their trigger into a spectacle through your own reaction. Loud concern, dramatic fussing, announcing to the room that something is wrong, all of it amplifies the exposure you are trying to reduce. Calm and low-key is the whole aesthetic. You want your partner to be able to look back on the moment and feel that they were quietly and competently held, not that they became a scene. And afterward, resist the urge to make the public setting into a reason they should explain themselves. They do not owe the restaurant, or you, an account. They owe themselves a soft landing, and your job is to make the exit from a public space feel like protection rather than escort.

This is not therapy, and you are not the therapist

I have to underline the boundary this chapter lives inside, because the Four-Step Pause can fool you into thinking you have become your partner's treatment. You have not. Being a steady presence during a trigger is ordinary partnership, the same thing a good friend would offer, and it is not clinical care. You are not equipped to treat trauma, and you should not try, and the ongoing work of healing the triggers belongs to your partner and their own support, a therapist, a practice, a process that is theirs.

This matters for your own sake as much as theirs. If you take on the job of managing your partner's triggers, tracking their landmines, arranging the world to prevent their reactions, you will slide into a hypervigilance of your own, the eggshell-walking this book keeps warning against, and you will lose yourself in a role no partner should carry. Your job during a trigger is presence, and your job the rest of the time is not trigger-prevention. It is to live your shared life normally, to treat your partner as a capable adult with their own support rather than a fragile thing you must protect from the world. The steady presence is a gift. The full-time management is a trap, and the difference between them is the difference between a partner and a caretaker.

There is a fair question hiding here that this book will not dodge: how often is too often? A trigger now and then, handled with a pause and followed by return and repair, is simply part of dating someone with trauma, and it asks something reasonable of you. A partner who is triggered constantly, whose reactions fill most of your time together, who is not engaged in any of their own healing work, is a different situation, and one that can quietly consume you. Noticing frequency is not cruelty. It is one of the pieces of information you will need for the larger decision later in this book, about whether the relationship as it actually is fits the life you actually want. For now, hold the presence lightly and openly, offering it freely while keeping your eyes open.

The action: rehearse the pause

Here is your work this week, and you do it alone, before you ever need it, because you cannot learn a new response in the middle of a crisis. Rehearse the Four-Step Pause in your imagination. Picture a moment where your partner gets triggered, and walk yourself through it. Notice. Steady yourself, one slow breath, this is a wave not an emergency. Offer with options, would quiet help, close or some room. Stay. Run it a few times, until the sequence feels available rather than foreign. And separately, at a calm moment with your partner, you can ask the one genuinely useful advance question: when you are having a hard moment, is there anything that tends to help, or anything I should not do? Whatever they say, believe them, and let their answer, not your instinct to fix, be your guide. You are not preparing to rescue anyone. You are preparing to be steady, which is the only thing that was ever yours to offer, and which turns out to be enough. You will not do this perfectly, and you do not need to. A triggered person does not require a flawless responder who says the ideal thing at the ideal moment. They require a present one, someone who did not flee and did not flood, someone who stayed steady while the wave passed. Aim for present, not perfect, and forgive yourself the moments you get it wrong, because the staying matters far more than the precision, and a partner who is human and reliable is worth more than one who is polished and absent. Steady and human will always be worth more to a frightened body than polished and far away. That steadiness is also the ground the next chapter stands on, when the question stops being how to get through a hard moment and becomes how to commit without disappearing into each other.

Chapter 8: Exclusivity Without Fusion

Two couples, same milestone. Lysant and her partner decided to be exclusive after three months, and the decision changed almost nothing about their days. They still had their own friends, their own weeknights, their own ambitions. What changed was a quiet agreement to build toward each other on purpose. Valenor and his partner decided to be exclusive after eleven days, and the decision changed everything. Within weeks they had merged their whole lives, spoke of each other as their entire world, dropped their friends, and described the intensity as proof of how rare this was. One of these is commitment. The other is fusion, and this chapter is about telling them apart, because they can feel identical from the inside and they lead to completely different places.

Exclusivity is a healthy, ordinary step toward building something real. Fusion, two people collapsing into one, losing their separate selves in the name of love, is not a deeper version of commitment. It is a different and more fragile thing, and with a trauma-affected partner it carries specific risks worth naming clearly.

Commitment and fusion are not the same thing

Commitment says: I am choosing you, and we are two whole people building a life alongside each other. Fusion says: I am dissolving into you, and we are becoming one thing, and the separateness that used to define us is the enemy of our love. The words can sound similar. The structure is opposite. Commitment preserves two selves and joins them. Fusion erases two selves and replaces them with a merged unit that has no room for the individuals inside it.

Fusion feels wonderful at first, which is exactly why it is dangerous. The loss of self reads as romantic intensity, the world narrowing to just the two of you feels like depth, and the abandonment of your outside life feels like devotion. But a self that has been dissolved cannot show up for a relationship, because there is no one left to show up. Over time, fusion breeds resentment, because needs do not actually disappear when you pretend to have none, and it breeds fragility, because a merged unit cannot survive the ordinary separateness that real life requires. The couples who last are not the ones who became one person. They are the ones who stayed two people who chose each other.

The Two Whole Lives

Here is the principle. The Two Whole Lives: the goal is not to merge two people into one life, but to keep two whole lives that increasingly overlap by choice. Commitment deepens the overlap. It does not erase the two lives. You want more shared territory over time, and you want each person to remain a person, with their own friends, their own interests, their own separate existence that does not require the other's permission or presence.

This is not a lukewarm, keep-your-distance philosophy. It is the opposite. Two whole lives that overlap by choice is a stronger, warmer thing than one fused blob, because the overlap is chosen freshly, again and again, rather than enforced by the absence of any alternative. When you keep your own life and still choose your partner every day, that choice means something, because you could do otherwise and you do not. When you have dissolved your life entirely, the choosing stops, because there is nothing left to choose from. Attachment research is relevant here: the most secure bonds are ones where each person can move toward closeness and back toward autonomy freely, using the relationship as a base to return to rather than a cage to be locked inside (Mikulincer & Shaver, 2016). The base works precisely because it is not a cage.

Why fusion is riskier with a trauma-affected partner

Fusion is unhealthy for anyone, but it carries extra hazards here, in two directions. In one direction, a trauma-affected partner may find rapid fusion overwhelming, because the loss of autonomy can feel like a threat to a system that already struggles with safety and control, and so the very intensity that feels like love to you can quietly alarm them. In the other direction, if your partner is the one pushing for rapid fusion, that push can be a way of managing their own fear, an attempt to secure you completely and immediately so the uncertainty of a normal-paced relationship does not have to be tolerated. Neither of these is a character flaw. Both are reasons to keep the Two Whole Lives in view rather than surrendering to the pull.

There is also the accommodation trap from earlier chapters, which fusion accelerates. When you dissolve your life into your partner's, you are perfectly positioned to reorganize everything around their comfort, their avoidance, their needs, until the merged unit runs entirely on their nervous system's terms and yours has vanished. Research on couples affected by trauma links exactly this kind of accommodation, reshaping your life around a partner's distress, to worse outcomes over time (Fredman et al., 2014). Keeping your own whole life is not selfishness. It is the structural protection against becoming a caretaker in a costume of romance.

The love-bomb line

Now the hardest distinction in this chapter, and I want to draw it carefully, because it can be misused. There is a pattern sometimes called love-bombing: intense, rapid, overwhelming displays of affection and commitment very early, a flood of attention and future-talk and declarations, moving to fuse fast and hard. Sometimes this is simply an anxious, fast-moving person, or a genuinely smitten one, and it settles into something healthy. Sometimes it is the opening move of a controlling dynamic, where the early flood is a way of securing power, and it is later followed by withdrawal of that affection as a means of control. You cannot tell which from the intensity alone, and you should not try to diagnose it. What you can do is watch what happens when you keep your own life.

Here is the line, and it is a behavioral test, not a label. When you maintain your separateness, see your friends, keep your routines, decline to fuse on command, how does your partner respond? A healthy fast-mover may be disappointed but respects it, and adjusts. A controlling dynamic tends to escalate, to treat your autonomy as betrayal, to guilt or pressure or punish you for keeping a life of your own. The intensity is not the signal. The response to your boundaries is the signal. Someone who loves you wants you to remain a whole person. Someone who wants to control you experiences your wholeness as a threat.

Valenor learned this from the inside, as the one who had been fusing. He had believed the eleven-day exclusivity and the total merging were proof of a once-in-a-lifetime love. What he could not see, until it collapsed, was that the fusion had left him with no separate ground to stand on when the relationship turned controlling, and it did turn, the early flood giving way to jealousy about the friends he no longer saw and the life he no longer had. He rebuilt slowly, and in his next relationship he did something that felt frightening at first. He kept his own life. And the keeping of it was the thing that finally let him tell, early, whether a partner respected him or wanted to absorb him.

The myth that intensity is evidence

The belief running under fusion is that intensity is evidence, that the sheer force of early feeling proves the relationship is real and rare and meant to be. It is worth pulling this belief apart, because it is doing a lot of damage quietly. Intensity is a feeling, and feelings are real, but a feeling is not evidence about the thing that caused it. Early intensity can come from genuine compatibility, and it can equally come from anxiety, from novelty, from the nervous system's alarm being mistaken for excitement, from two people's fears fitting together in a way that feels like destiny and is actually just a lock and a key. The intensity tells you something is happening. It does not tell you what.

This matters because the intensity myth makes people override their own judgment. A warning sign appears, and the intensity says but it feels so strong, this must be real, and the judgment gets silenced by the feeling. With a trauma-affected partner, or a trauma-affected you, the intensity can be especially high and especially misleading, because heightened arousal of any kind, including fear, can read as passion. So hold intensity lightly as information. Enjoy it, do not worship it, and never let it be your evidence. The evidence you actually want is slower and quieter: how does this person treat you across many ordinary days, especially the ones that go wrong. That evidence accumulates whether or not the fireworks are loud, and it is the only kind that predicts anything.

Milestones without merging

Commitment involves milestones, exclusivity, meeting each other's people, spending more nights together, eventually perhaps sharing a home, and each of these can be taken as an overlap of two whole lives or as another step of fusion. The milestone itself is neutral. What matters is whether you keep yourselves as you take it. You can become exclusive and keep your friends. You can meet the family and keep your weeknights. You can spend most nights together and keep some that are your own. The milestones deepen the overlap without dissolving the two people, which is exactly what you want.

The trap is treating each milestone as a mandate to merge further, so that exclusivity is supposed to mean losing your independent social life, and sharing a home is supposed to mean sharing every hour. It is not, and the couples who understand this build in separateness on purpose even as they build togetherness. They keep a night, a friendship, a corner of life that is theirs. This is not a hedge against the relationship, and it is not a lack of commitment. It is the thing that keeps the commitment healthy, because a person who has kept themselves has something to bring, and a person who has dissolved has only need. Take the milestones. Take them gladly. Just carry both whole lives across each threshold, rather than leaving one of them behind at the door.

There is a conversation that makes this easier, and it is worth having out loud as the milestones approach. You can say, plainly and warmly, that you want to build toward each other and you also want you both to stay whole, and ask what each of you needs to protect as things get more serious. That conversation reframes independence as something you are protecting together, rather than something one of you is defending against the other. It turns the keeping of separate lives into a shared value instead of a point of tension, which is exactly what it should be.

When you are the one who wants to fuse

It is worth turning this on yourself, because the pull to fuse is often ours, not only our partner's. If you lean anxious in attachment, the early weeks can make you want to merge fast, to secure the relationship by dissolving the gaps, to quiet your fear of losing them by making yourselves into one thing that cannot come apart (Mikulincer & Shaver, 2016). That urge is understandable and it is worth resisting, because fusion does not actually secure anything. It just removes the vantage point from which you could tell whether the relationship deserves securing.

If you notice the urge, the move is not to suppress your love but to route your energy back into your own whole life. Keep the friends. Keep the interests. Let the relationship deepen at the speed of actual knowledge rather than the speed of your fear. Choosing your partner from a full life is a stronger act of love than needing them from an empty one, and it is also, not incidentally, far more attractive. Wholeness is magnetic. Desperation, however romantic it feels from the inside, is not.

Lysant, by contrast, never had to unlearn fusion, because she had built her exclusivity on two whole lives from the start. When she and her partner committed, the commitment was an overlap, not an erasure. They saw each other more, chose each other more, wove their lives together more, and each of them remained entirely a person. It was less intense, at first, than the fused version other couples described. It was also still standing, and deepening, long after the intense fusions around them had burned out. She had traded the fireworks for a fire, and the fire kept them warm.

If keeping yourself causes friction

Sometimes keeping your own life will bump against your partner, and it helps to know in advance what that friction does and does not mean. If your partner feels a little insecure when you keep a night with friends, and says so, and can be reassured, that is ordinary and workable. Insecurity is not the same as control. You can hold your separateness and hold their feelings at the same time, reassuring them of your commitment while still keeping the night. Care about the feeling, keep the boundary. Both.

What is not workable, over time, is a pattern where any separateness is treated as betrayal, where your keeping a life of your own reliably produces guilt trips, escalation, or punishment. That is the love-bomb line showing itself in a new setting, and it is worth watching without rushing to a verdict. One anxious reaction is a feeling to be soothed. A steady pattern of your wholeness being treated as a threat is information for the larger decision this book builds toward. In the meantime, keep the thing that is yours, respond to insecurity with warmth rather than surrender, and notice, across time, whether your separateness is met with respect or resistance. The answer to that question will tell you more than any declaration of love ever could.

The action: keep one whole thing

Here is your work this week. Identify one part of your own life that is entirely yours, a friendship, a practice, a routine, an interest, something that predates this relationship and does not require your partner, and protect it, deliberately, this week. Do the thing. See the friend. Keep the evening. Not as a message to your partner, and not as a test, but as a practice of remaining a whole person while you build toward someone. Then notice, quietly, how it feels to keep it, and, if it comes up, how your partner responds to your keeping it. You are not building a wall. You are keeping the ground you stand on, the separate life from which real choosing becomes possible. Exclusivity is a fine and good step. Just make sure that when you take it, there are still two of you left to take it, because everything worth building needs two whole people to build it, and the next chapter is about protecting the wholeness that is specifically yours.

Chapter 9: Staying Yourself

There is a moment I want you to catch before it catches you. It is the moment you realize you have not thought about your own day in weeks, because every ounce of your attention has been going toward monitoring theirs. You know their moods better than your own. You have not seen your friends. You have started editing yourself before you speak, running each sentence through a filter of will this be too much for them. You have become, without deciding to, the supportive one, and somewhere in becoming that, you have quietly stopped being you.

This chapter is the one I most want you to take seriously, because everything else in this book fails if you disappear. You cannot date at a sustainable pace from inside a self that no longer exists. You cannot offer steady presence if you are running on empty. And you cannot make a good decision about the relationship, the decision the last chapters build toward, if there is no longer a you left with needs and preferences to consult. Staying yourself is not the selfish part of trauma-aware dating. It is the load-bearing part.

How good people erase themselves

Self-erasure rarely arrives as a dramatic sacrifice. It arrives as a thousand small, reasonable-seeming accommodations, each one defensible, that add up to a person who has vanished. You stop mentioning your hard day because theirs was harder. You stop asking for the closeness you want because they need space. You cancel your plans because they are struggling. You shrink your own needs because voicing them feels like adding to a load that is already heavy. Each choice looks like kindness. The sum is a slow disappearing.

The mechanism has a name in the research, and seeing it named helps. Partner accommodation is the way loved ones reshape their own behavior to reduce a partner's distress, and studies of couples affected by trauma find that high accommodation is associated with worse relationship functioning over time, not better (Fredman et al., 2014). This is counterintuitive and important. The very self-erasure that feels like devotion tends to degrade the relationship, because a relationship needs two people in it, and accommodation quietly removes one of them. When you reorganize your entire self around your partner's symptoms, you do not build a stronger bond. You build a caretaking arrangement, and caretaking arrangements breed the resentment and distance that eventually corrode everything.

The Anchor Rule

Here is the principle, and it is the one to tattoo somewhere you will see it. The Anchor Rule: you cannot be a steady anchor for anyone if you have pulled up your own anchor to drift with them. Your groundedness, your separate life, your own needs and friends and sense of self, these are not obstacles to supporting your partner. They are the thing that makes support possible. An anchor works because it is fixed to the seabed. Pull it up to follow the current, and you are just another thing being swept along.

This reframes staying yourself from an act of selfishness into an act of service, though I would rather you did it simply because you deserve to exist. When you keep your own life, you have something to give. When you keep your own needs, you can offer candor instead of a slow-building resentment. When you keep your own friends, you have support that is not your struggling partner, so you are not asking them to be your whole world at the moment they can least be anyone's whole world. The grounded partner is the useful partner. The dissolved partner is a liability wearing the mask of a saint.

Éloane, thirty-five, learned this at the bottom of it. She had spent the better part of a year becoming the perfect support for a partner in a hard stretch, and she had been proud of it, right up until she noticed she could not remember the last time she had wanted anything for herself. She had no plans, no friends she still saw, no opinions she still voiced, no interests she still pursued. She had become an extension of his recovery, and the strange, awful part was that it had not even helped him, because he did not want an extension, he wanted a person, and she had stopped being one. Her recovery of herself was not graceful. It started with one reclaimed evening and a friend she had to apologize to for disappearing. But it saved both her and, as it turned out, the relationship, because the moment she started being a person again was the moment they had something real between them instead of a patient and his attendant.

Your needs are not a burden

The belief that keeps people erasing themselves is that their needs are a burden, that a partner with trauma is already carrying so much that adding your needs would be cruel. This belief is wrong, and it is worth dismantling directly, because it drives so much of the damage. Your partner is a whole adult, not a fragile object, and treating their capacity as so limited that they cannot hear your needs is its own quiet insult. It casts them as an invalid and you as their nurse, and most people with trauma do not want that role for you any more than you should want it for yourself.

Your needs are not a burden. They are the normal requirements of a person in a relationship, and a relationship that cannot hold both people's needs is not actually holding either. Voicing your needs is not adding to your partner's load. It is refusing to build a relationship on the fiction that you do not exist. And here is the part that surprises people: partners with trauma often feel relieved to be given your needs, because it means they are being treated as a partner capable of showing up, rather than a patient who must be protected from the demands of a real relationship. Alven found exactly this. He had spent months in a relationship where his partner never asked him for anything, and he had slowly come to feel like a project rather than a person, someone to be managed rather than loved. When she finally started telling him what she needed, he was not burdened. He was grateful, because for the first time she was treating him like someone who could give, not just someone who had to be carefully handled.

Warning signs you are disappearing

It helps to have a few concrete markers, because self-erasure is hard to see from inside. Watch for these. You cannot remember the last time you asked for something for yourself. Your friends have started commenting on your absence, or you have started avoiding them because explaining feels like too much. You filter your speech constantly, pre-screening your own words for their impact before you dare say anything true. Your moods have become entirely dependent on theirs, so that you cannot be okay unless they are okay. You have stopped doing the things that used to be yours, and you cannot quite say when you stopped.

None of these makes you a failure, and noticing them is not an indictment. It is the beginning of coming back. The presence of these signs does not mean the relationship is wrong, necessarily. It means you have drifted, and drifting is reversible, and the reversing starts the moment you notice. But it does have to start, because a self left to erode long enough does not simply spring back, and a relationship built on your disappearance was never going to hold anyway.

Supporting and rescuing are different jobs

There is a distinction underneath this whole chapter that is worth making sharp, because people collapse the two and lose themselves in the confusion. Supporting a partner and rescuing a partner look similar from a distance and are opposite in practice. Supporting means being present and caring while your partner does their own work and lives their own life. Rescuing means trying to do their work for them, to carry what is theirs, to manage their internal state so they do not have to. Support keeps two adults in the room. Rescue quietly demotes one of them to a patient and installs you as staff.

You can feel the difference in your own body if you pay attention. Support feels sustainable, warm, and mutual, a thing you can do for years without corroding. Rescue feels urgent, heavy, and depleting, a thing that takes more from you each week and never quite arrives at enough. When you catch yourself in the rescue posture, scanning for their moods, arranging the world to prevent their distress, absorbing responsibility for feelings that are not yours, that is the signal to step back and hand the work back to the person it belongs to. Not coldly. You can be warm and still refuse a job that is not yours. In fact the warmest thing you can do for a partner with trauma is to treat them as capable of their own recovery, because the alternative, treating them as too fragile to carry their own life, is a subtle way of telling them you do not believe they can heal. Support believes in them. Rescue, however tender, does not.

Coming back after you have drifted

If you read the warning signs and recognized yourself, you are not too late, and the way back is more ordinary than you fear. You do not have to blow up the relationship or announce a dramatic transformation. You rebuild a self the same way you lost it, one small choice at a time, in the other direction. Where self-erasure was a thousand tiny surrenders, recovery is a thousand tiny reclamations, and the first few are the hardest because the muscle has gone weak.

Start absurdly small, small enough that you cannot talk yourself out of it. One preference voiced out loud. One evening kept. One friend contacted. One true thing said without the reflexive apology. Each small reclamation rebuilds the muscle a little, and the muscle is the thing, not any single act. Expect it to feel uncomfortable, even selfish, at first, because a self that has been trained to disappear experiences its own reappearance as a transgression. That discomfort is not a sign you are doing something wrong. It is the sensation of a boundary being rebuilt after long neglect, and it fades as the self returns.

Expect, too, that your partner may notice the shift and have feelings about it, and hold steady through that. If the relationship is healthy, your reappearance will ultimately be welcomed, because your partner would rather have a whole person than a ghost, even if the adjustment takes a moment. If your becoming a person again is met with sustained resistance, if your having needs is treated as a problem to be suppressed, that is not a reason to disappear again. It is information, and it belongs to the decision the next chapters are building toward. Either way, the instruction is the same. Come back. Reclaim the self, small choice by small choice, and refuse to trade your existence for anyone's comfort, because the whole point of building a relationship is to have a life inside it, and there is no life where there is no you.

The myth that love means putting them first

The belief that licenses all of this disappearing is a romantic one, which is why it is so hard to question. Love, we are told, means putting the other person first, and so putting yourself second, and then third, and then nowhere, can feel like the very proof of how much you care. Held up to the light, the belief falls apart, because a relationship in which one person is always first is not a relationship, it is a hierarchy, and hierarchies do not produce intimacy, they produce a servant and a served. Real love is not one person perpetually yielding to the other. It is two people who both matter, taking turns, holding each other's needs alongside their own.

Putting your partner first as an occasional, chosen act, on a hard night, in a real crisis, is generous and good. Putting your partner first as a permanent policy, so that your needs are structurally subordinate to theirs, is not love, it is self-erasure with a noble name, and it curdles. The partner who is always put first does not feel more loved over time. They feel increasingly alone, because there is no equal in the room to be loved by, only an attendant anticipating their needs. And the partner who always yields does not feel more virtuous over time. They feel invisible, and eventually resentful, and the resentment leaks out sideways in ways that damage everyone.

So retire the myth, and replace it with something sturdier. Love means both of you matter, and a relationship worth building is one where your needs and theirs sit at the same table. That is not a lesser love than the self-sacrificing kind. It is a truer one, and it is the only kind that lasts, because it does not require anyone to disappear to sustain it.

The action: reclaim one thing that is yours

Here is your work this week, and it is the most important assignment in this book. Reclaim one thing that is genuinely yours and that you have let go. Not for your partner, not as a message, not as a test. For you, because you are a person who deserves to keep existing. Call the friend you have not seen. Go back to the thing you loved before this relationship swallowed your calendar. Say one true thing about your own day, your own need, your own preference, out loud, to your partner, and let it simply be true without apologizing for it. Then notice how it feels to take up space again, and notice, too, that the relationship did not end because you became a person in it. If anything ends because you refuse to disappear, it was going to end anyway, and better now than after you have vanished completely. You are allowed to stay yourself. In fact you are required to, because the person your partner deserves to be dating, and the person who gets to decide whether this relationship is worth building, is you, whole and present and still here. The self you keep is not a wall you build against your partner. It is the gift you bring them, the whole person they get to love instead of the ghost they would otherwise have to manage. Stay whole for both of you, and refuse, gently and permanently, to mistake your own disappearance for devotion. No relationship worth keeping ever required you to vanish in order to keep it. You get to exist inside your own love story, not merely staff it from the wings. Hold onto that person. Everything left in this book depends on it.

Chapter 10: Red Flag or Trauma Response

Here is the same scene, read two ways. Your partner snaps at you, cold and cutting, over something small. Reading one: they are overwhelmed, their history is loud today, this is a trauma response and it deserves patience. Reading two: this is how they handle not getting their way, a flash of contempt that will become a pattern, and this is a red flag you should not excuse. The behavior is identical. The two readings lead to opposite lives. And the question that keeps you up at night, the one this whole book has been circling, is how on earth you are supposed to tell which one you are looking at.

This is the hardest chapter to write, because it sits on a knife edge. Lean one way and you teach people to excuse genuine mistreatment as trauma, which traps them in harm. Lean the other and you teach people to read every wound as a warning sign, which makes them abandon good partners for being human. I am going to give you a way through that does not require you to diagnose anyone, because you cannot, and should not, and it would not help anyway. The way through is not about labeling the behavior. It is about watching what happens after.

Why you cannot sort this by the behavior alone

Start by giving up the thing you most want, which is a checklist of behaviors that are trauma responses and behaviors that are red flags. It does not exist, and every version of it lies to you, because the same surface behavior can come from opposite places. Withdrawal can be a nervous system seeking safety, or it can be stonewalling used to punish. Anger can be a flooded system, or it can be intimidation. Jealousy can be an attachment wound, or it can be the first bars of a cage. You cannot read the source from the surface, and trying to turns you into an amateur diagnostician sorting your partner's every act into folders you are not qualified to label.

So stop trying to classify the behavior in the moment, and start watching the pattern over time, because the pattern is where the truth lives. A single cold remark tells you almost nothing. What tells you everything is what your partner does with that remark across the following hours and days, and whether the same harm keeps happening no matter what. Herman's foundational work on trauma and abuse drew a clear line here: coercive control is defined not by isolated incidents but by a sustained pattern that erodes a person's autonomy and reality over time (Herman, 1992). The pattern, not the incident, is the unit of meaning. And the single most revealing feature of the pattern is whether it includes repair.

The Repair Test

Here is the principle, and it is the most useful tool in this book for the question you fear most. The Repair Test: you cannot tell a red flag from a trauma response by the behavior, but you can tell a great deal by what follows it, because a trauma response tends to be followed, eventually, by awareness, ownership, and repair, while a red flag tends to be followed by denial, blame, and repetition. Do not read the wound. Read the aftermath.

Watch for the shape of what comes after harm. When someone's difficult behavior comes from a trauma response, and they are doing their own work, the arc bends toward repair. They may not manage it in the moment, but later they come back. They recognize what happened. They own their part without drowning you in it. They can say some version of I am sorry, that was mine, not yours, and here is what I am trying to do about it. And, crucially, over time, the harm reduces, because they are working on it. Repair is present, accountability is present, and the pattern is improving, not entrenching.

When difficult behavior is a red flag, the arc bends the other way. After the harm comes denial that it happened, or blame that reassigns it to you, that says you made me do it, you are too sensitive, this is your fault. There is no genuine ownership, only the performance of an apology that changes nothing, or an apology that becomes its own weapon. And the pattern repeats, or worsens, regardless of how much patience and understanding you offer. No repair, no accountability, no change, or change that lasts only until the next cycle. That absence is the signal, and it is a signal you can read without diagnosing anyone, because you are not judging their inner condition, you are observing whether harm is followed by repair.

Virel, thirty-three, used the Repair Test to save a good relationship he had almost thrown away. His partner would sometimes go sharp and distant under stress, and Virel, primed by dating advice to spot red flags, kept bracing to leave. What the Repair Test showed him, when he actually watched the aftermath instead of the incident, was a consistent arc toward repair. She always came back. She owned it. She named what had happened and what she was working on. The harm was real but it was decreasing, and it was always followed by accountability. That was not a red flag. That was a person with a trauma response doing her work, and the behavior he had been ready to flee was, read across time, a sign of health, not danger.

When the test reveals a red flag

The Repair Test cuts the other way too, and this is the part I need you to take seriously, because trauma-aware people are especially vulnerable to missing it. Noélin, thirty-one, spent a long time excusing a partner's contempt, jealousy, and control as trauma responses, because the partner genuinely had a serious history and Noélin did not want to be the person who punished someone for being wounded. The trauma was real. But when she finally applied the Repair Test squarely, the aftermath told a consistent story: no ownership, blame that always landed on her, apologies that were really demands for sympathy, and a pattern that did not improve no matter how much she understood, accommodated, and forgave. It got worse.

Here is the sentence Noélin needed, and it is the spine of this chapter. A trauma history explains a behavior. It does not excuse harm, and it does not obligate you to keep absorbing it. Both things are true at once. Her partner's history was real and deserved compassion, and her partner's treatment of her was harmful and she did not have to stay for it. Understanding where a behavior comes from is an act of empathy. Accepting ongoing harm because you understand its origin is a different act, and it is not required of you, ever. Compassion for someone's wounds and refusal to be wounded by them are not in conflict. You can hold both, and when the Repair Test comes back with no repair, no accountability, and a worsening pattern, holding both means you can leave with compassion, which is exactly what Noélin finally did.

The line that is never a trauma response

There is one place where the whole framework of this chapter stops applying, and I have to be completely clear about it, because ambiguity here is dangerous. Nothing in this book, and nothing about trauma, ever excuses abuse. If there is physical violence, or threats, or a pattern of coercive control that isolates you, monitors you, degrades you, and strips away your autonomy, you are not looking at a puzzle to be solved with patience and repair tests. Coercive control is a pattern that erodes a person's freedom and sense of reality, and it is defined by that erosion, not by the presence or absence of a trauma history in the person doing it (Herman, 1992). A trauma history does not make abuse into something else. Abuse is abuse, and your safety comes before your compassion, always, without exception.

If you recognize this, the Repair Test is not the tool you need. The tool you need is support from outside the relationship, a domestic violence hotline, a trusted person, a professional, someone who can help you think clearly from a position of safety. In the United States, the National Domestic Violence Hotline is available around the clock. Please do not use the ideas in this book to talk yourself into staying somewhere unsafe. Understanding is not the same as endangering yourself, and no amount of empathy for someone's past obligates you to remain in harm's present.

The two traps, and which one is yours

There are two ways to get this question wrong, and knowing which one you personally lean toward is half the battle. The first trap is over-excusing, treating every harmful behavior as a trauma response to be endured, so that a person's history becomes a permanent hall pass for how they treat you. This is the trap that trauma-aware people fall into most, precisely because they are compassionate and informed. You know about nervous systems and triggers and the body keeping the score, and that knowledge, aimed the wrong way, becomes a sophisticated machine for explaining away your own mistreatment. The more you understand, the better you can rationalize staying.

The second trap is over-diagnosing, reading every wound as a red flag, bracing for danger at every ordinary human failure, so that a good partner having a hard day gets filed as a threat and abandoned. This trap catches people who have been hurt before and are determined never to be hurt again, and it costs them relationships that were actually healthy, because no real person can pass a test that treats every imperfection as evidence of danger.

The Repair Test threads between both, because it does not ask you to excuse or to accuse. It asks you to watch. Over-excusing ignores the absence of repair and stays anyway. Over-diagnosing ignores the presence of repair and leaves anyway. The test simply asks you to notice which one is actually happening, across time, and to let that observation, rather than your fear or your hope, guide you. If you know you lean toward excusing, watch the aftermath more clearly than your compassion wants to. If you know you lean toward diagnosing, watch it more patiently than your fear wants to. Either way, watch, and let what you actually see be the thing you trust.

How long do you give it

A fair question follows from all this: how long do you watch before the pattern counts as a pattern? There is no exact number, and anyone who gives you one is selling certainty they do not have. But there are reliable guideposts. A pattern is not one incident, so you do not decide anything from a single hard moment. A pattern is also not endless, so you do not get to keep watching forever as a way of avoiding a decision you are afraid of. Somewhere between those, across enough repetitions that a genuine shape emerges, the aftermath will start telling you the same story again and again, and when it does, believe it.

Two cautions about time. Do not use patience as a way to postpone a truth you already see. Trauma-aware people are experts at giving it more time, and sometimes more time is wisdom and sometimes it is avoidance wearing wisdom's clothes. If the aftermath has shown you no repair and a worsening pattern across many cycles, more time is not going to reveal a repair that has never once appeared. And on the other side, do not demand that a pattern prove itself instantly. Repair sometimes shows up slowly, especially early, when a person is still learning to come back at all. Give the aftermath a real chance to appear before you conclude it is absent. The skill is watching long enough to see the true shape, and not so long that you have quietly agreed to accept whatever the shape turns out to be. Your safety and your self-respect set the outer limit. Within it, watch closely, and trust what you see.

The action: watch one aftermath

Here is your work, and it is patient observation, not confrontation. The next time something difficult happens between you, a snap, a withdrawal, a cold moment, do not rush to classify it as a trauma response or a red flag. Instead, watch the aftermath, and notice three things across the following hours and days. Does your partner come to any awareness of what happened. Do they take ownership without turning it back on you. And, over time, across many such moments, is the pattern getting better or worse. Write down what you observe, plainly, without the story you want to be true and without the catastrophe you fear. You are not diagnosing anyone. You are reading the aftermath, which is the one thing you can actually read, and letting the presence or absence of repair tell you what the behavior alone never could. Keep the observation private and truthful, and give it enough time to show a real shape without giving it so much time that watching becomes a way of not deciding. If what you see is repair, accountability, and a pattern that improves, you are likely looking at a person doing their work, and the difficulty is worth your patience. If what you see is denial, blame, and a pattern that entrenches, you are looking at something else, and your compassion for its origins does not require you to keep living inside its consequences. None of this is about becoming suspicious of the person you love, scanning them for evidence, quietly building a case against them. It is about staying clear-eyed with yourself in a situation designed to confuse you, where compassion and self-protection can feel like enemies and are not. You can hold enormous tenderness for where your partner's difficult behavior comes from and still insist, without apology, that harm be met with repair. Those two things are not in conflict. They are the two hands of loving someone with trauma while remaining a whole person yourself, one hand open in understanding, the other steady on the line you will not cross. Read the aftermath, believe what it shows you across time rather than what you wish it showed, and let it, not your hope and not your fear, tell you whether the difficulty in front of you is a wound in the process of healing or a wound being handed to you again and again. Trust the pattern over the promise, and trust it over your own fear as well, because the aftermath, watched across time, does not lie the way a single moment can. That reading is not the whole decision about whether to stay, but it is one of its foundations, and the next chapter adds another, watching what happens in the place where every couple is eventually tested, the first real conflict.

Chapter 11: What the First Conflict Reveals

The first real disagreement was about something small, which is how it usually goes. Sorell and her partner had different ideas about a weekend, said so, and felt the temperature in the room change. It was not a screaming fight. It was the first time they had wanted different things out loud and had to do something about it. And in the twenty minutes that followed, Sorell learned more about whether this relationship could last than she had learned in the previous three months of good dates, because the good dates had never tested the one thing that actually predicts a future, which is not whether you fight but whether you can find your way back.

This chapter is about that first conflict, and why you should almost welcome it. Couples who never disagree are not more compatible. They are usually more frightened, avoiding the conflict that would reveal whether they can survive it. The first real disagreement is not a failure of the relationship. It is the relationship finally showing you its most important feature, and with a trauma-affected partner, that feature is often obscured by a specific fear you need to understand.

Conflict avoidance is not peace

For many trauma survivors, conflict does not register as an ordinary disagreement. It registers as danger, because somewhere in their history conflict preceded harm, and the body learned that raised voices or disagreement mean threat. So a trauma-affected partner may avoid conflict intensely, going silent, agreeing to things they do not agree with, changing the subject, disappearing rather than disagreeing. From the outside this can look like an easy, harmonious relationship, and you can mistake the absence of conflict for the presence of peace.

It is not peace. It is avoidance, and avoidance is expensive, because the disagreements do not vanish when they are suppressed. They accumulate. The needs that go unspoken do not stop existing. They pool, quietly, under the smooth surface, until the surface cannot hold them, and then they surface sideways, as resentment, as distance, as a sudden rupture that seems to come from nowhere but was actually built from everything that was never said. Research on couples affected by trauma consistently ties poor communication, the inability to raise and work through disagreement, to lower relationship satisfaction over time (Campbell & Renshaw, 2012). A relationship where conflict is forbidden is not safe. It is a relationship where problems have nowhere to go.

The Repair Signal

Here is the principle for this chapter. The Repair Signal: what predicts a relationship's future is not whether the two of you fight, but whether you can repair, and the first conflict is your first real reading of that signal. Every couple disagrees. The couples who last are not the ones who disagree least. They are the ones who, after disagreeing, can find their way back to each other, and the first conflict is where you get to see whether that capacity exists between you.

Watch for the repair, in both directions. When the disagreement happens, does someone reach back across the gap? A repair attempt can be small and clumsy, a joke to break the tension, a hand extended, an I hate this, can we start over, an okay, I hear you. It does not have to be elegant. It just has to be an attempt to reconnect rather than to win or to flee. And, just as important, watch how repair attempts are received. A relationship where one person reaches back and the other accepts the reach, even imperfectly, has the thing that matters. A relationship where repair attempts are refused, where the reach is met with more coldness, more withdrawal, more punishment, is missing the one capacity a future depends on.

Sorell watched this in her twenty minutes. The disagreement itself was uncomfortable, but what she saw afterward reassured her more than any amount of harmony could have. Her partner, after a tense pause, reached back. He said some version of I do not want to fight about a weekend, your thing matters to me too, let us figure it out. It was not smooth. But it was a repair attempt, and Sorell met it, and together they found their way back, and in doing so they proved to each other that a disagreement did not have to become a catastrophe. That single successful repair told her more about their odds than everything that had come before.

How to have a first conflict well

You have some influence over how the first conflict goes, and it is worth using, not to avoid the conflict but to make it survivable. A few things help. Keep it about the actual issue rather than letting it balloon into a referendum on the whole relationship or on your partner's character. This weekend, this plan, this specific thing, not you always and you never. Stay in the disagreement without weaponizing your partner's trauma, never using what you know about their history as ammunition, never saying this is just your issues talking, which turns understanding into a weapon and violates everything this book stands for.

And make your own repair attempts, generously and early, especially since your partner may find them hard to initiate. You can be the one who reaches back first, who says I do not like this distance between us, who extends the hand. This is not the same as caving, as abandoning your position to make the discomfort stop, which is its own trauma-shaped move and helps no one. You can hold your actual need and reach for repair at the same time. I still think my thing matters, and I also do not want to be far from you right now, both. Modeling that combination, standing your ground and reaching back, teaches your partner that conflict does not have to mean either winning or vanishing, that there is a third option where two people disagree and stay connected.

Evanthe, twenty-eight, had to learn the difference between repair and capitulation the hard way. Her instinct in the first conflicts was to fold instantly, to abandon whatever she wanted the moment her partner tensed, because a tense partner frightened her and folding made the fear stop. She called it keeping the peace. What it actually was, she realized, was teaching both of them that her needs evaporated under pressure, which meant they never worked through anything, they just watched her disappear. Real repair, she learned, was harder and better. It meant staying in the disagreement long enough to actually resolve it, reaching for connection without surrendering herself. The first time she managed it, holding her position and reaching back at once, the conflict resolved for real instead of being buried, and she understood that she had been mistaking her own erasure for harmony for years.

The myth that good couples do not fight

The belief that keeps people avoiding conflict is that a good relationship is a conflict-free one, that if you were truly compatible you would not disagree, and so every disagreement is a small piece of evidence that something is wrong. This gets the truth almost exactly backwards. Two whole people with their own needs, histories, and preferences will inevitably want different things sometimes, and a relationship in which that never surfaces is not one without differences, it is one where the differences are being hidden. The absence of visible conflict is not a sign of compatibility. It is often a sign of suppression, and suppression has a cost that comes due later, with interest.

What actually distinguishes strong couples from fragile ones is not the frequency of conflict but the quality of repair. Strong couples fight and come back. Fragile couples either never fight, letting resentment accumulate in silence, or fight without any route back, letting each rupture harden into distance. So when the first disagreement arrives, resist the urge to read it as a bad sign. Read it instead as an opportunity, the first real chance to discover whether the two of you have the capacity that everything depends on. A relationship that can disagree and repair is not a flawed version of a conflict-free ideal. It is the actual healthy thing, and the conflict-free ideal is a fantasy that costs people their candor.

Repair does not have to happen in the moment

One thing that frees people up here: repair does not have to be immediate. In the heat of a disagreement, especially with a trauma-affected partner whose system may be flooded, neither of you may be capable of repair right then, and that is fine. What matters is that repair happens eventually, that the disagreement does not simply get buried and abandoned but gets returned to when both of you are calmer. Some of the most important repair happens hours or a day later, in the quiet after, when someone says that was hard, I do not like how we left it, can we talk.

This takes the pressure off the conflict itself. You do not have to resolve everything in the moment, and trying to force resolution while one or both of you is flooded usually makes things worse. You can agree, even in advance, that either of you can call a pause when things get too hot, on the condition that the pause is not the same as vanishing, that you will come back to it. A pause with a promise to return is regulation. A pause that becomes permanent silence is avoidance. The difference is whether the repair eventually arrives. If your partner needs to step away from a conflict and then reliably comes back to it when calm, that is a couple learning to fight well. If stepping away is how conflicts get disappeared forever, that is the avoidance this chapter warns about, and it is worth noticing which one is happening.

The reason this matters so much is that a couple who can repair after the fact has an almost unlimited capacity to handle hard things, because they know that no rupture is final, that there is always a way back. That knowledge, more than any communication technique, is what lets two people relax into a relationship. When you both trust that a fight will end in repair rather than in abandonment, conflict stops being terrifying, and a great deal of the walking-on-eggshells that haunts trauma-aware dating simply dissolves, because the thing you were afraid of, that a disagreement would end everything, has been proven false by experience.

When the first conflict reveals trouble

The Repair Signal can also come back negative, and you need to be willing to read it when it does. If the first real disagreement reveals that your partner cannot tolerate any conflict at all, that any disagreement sends them into a shutdown or a rage that does not resolve, that repair attempts are refused no matter how gently offered, that is important information, and it does not get better by being ignored. Some of this can shift with time and their own work, especially if the conflict-avoidance is trauma-shaped and they are actively working on it. But a relationship in which conflict can never happen and repair can never land is a relationship with no way to process the inevitable friction of two lives, and that is a structural problem, not a passing mood.

This connects directly to the Repair Test of the last chapter. There, you watched whether harm was followed by repair. Here, you watch whether conflict can reach repair at all. Both are asking the same underlying question from different angles: does this relationship have the capacity to rupture and mend, or only to rupture. A relationship that can mend can survive almost anything. A relationship that can only rupture, that has no route back after a disagreement, will eventually be undone by the ordinary conflicts that every couple faces, no matter how much the two people care.

When the avoidance is yours

It is easy to frame conflict-avoidance as your partner's issue, the trauma-shaped fear of disagreement, but be candid about your own side too, because dating someone with trauma can grow an avoidance in you that was not there before. You learn that your partner finds conflict hard, and out of care you start pre-avoiding it, swallowing your preferences, declining to raise the thing that bothers you, telling yourself you are being considerate. What you are often actually doing is protecting yourself from the discomfort of their reaction, and calling it kindness.

This is worth catching, because your avoidance and theirs can lock together into a relationship where nothing difficult is ever said by anyone, a perfect, silent, slowly poisoning peace. If you never raise your needs because you are afraid of how your partner will respond, you are not sparing them. You are denying them the chance to show you they can handle a real relationship, and you are denying yourself the chance to find out. Most partners with trauma are more capable than the eggshell-walking version of you assumes, and treating them as too fragile for an open disagreement is its own quiet condescension. The considerate move is not to hide your needs. It is to raise them kindly and give your partner the dignity of rising to meet them. Sometimes they will not manage it, and that is information. But you owe them the chance, and you owe yourself the candor, and a peace built on both of you disappearing was never worth keeping.

The action: let one small thing be a disagreement

Here is your work this week, and it may be the most counterintuitive assignment in the book. Do not manufacture a fight. But the next time you notice yourself about to fold, to swallow a real preference, to agree with something you do not actually agree with just to keep things smooth, do not fold. Say the true, small thing. I would actually prefer the other restaurant. That plan does not really work for me. Let there be a small, candid disagreement, and then, this is the important part, watch what happens. Does repair appear. Can the two of you disagree and find your way back. Reach back yourself, generously, and see if your reach is met. You are not testing your partner to trap them. You are gathering the single most predictive piece of information a relationship offers, which is not whether you can avoid conflict, but whether you can survive it together. A relationship that can rupture and mend is not a fragile thing pretending to be strong. It is the actual strong thing, tested and still standing, and it is worth far more than the frictionless quiet that never risked anything and never proved anything. Let the first conflict show you which of the two you have. No rupture is truly final in a couple that has learned the way back to each other. Everything that is left to decide rests on that answer, and deciding is exactly where this book goes last.

Chapter 12: Deciding Whether to Build

At some point the question stops being how to handle the silences or the triggers or the first conflict, and becomes the largest question of all, the one you have probably been carrying since the first chapter. Do I stay and build this, or do I go? Alaris sat with that question for a long month, and what made it so hard was not that the relationship was clearly bad, which would have made leaving simple, nor clearly good, which would have made staying simple. It was that it was genuinely mixed, real love tangled with real difficulty, and no amount of staring at it resolved into a verdict. This chapter is for that exact place, the crossroads where the answer is not obvious and you have to find a way to decide anyway.

I am not going to tell you what to do, because I cannot, and anyone who claims to know from the outside is guessing. What I can give you is a way to think that is clearer than the fog of hope and fear you are probably deciding in right now. It comes down to four things worth checking, four anchors that, held together, tell you more than any single good day or bad night ever could.

Why this decision is so hard

Before the framework, a word about why this is uniquely difficult, so you can be gentle with yourself for struggling. Dating someone with trauma layers a specific set of confusions onto an already hard decision. There is the guilt: leaving can feel like abandoning someone who is wounded, like punishing them for their history, and that guilt can keep you somewhere long past when you should have gone. There is the hope: you have seen who your partner is on the good days, and that glimpse of what could be can hold you through a great deal of what actually is. And there is the difficulty of separating the person from the pattern, of knowing whether you are in love with who they are or with who they might become if the trauma lifted.

All of this makes the decision murky, and the murk is where people get stuck for years. The four anchors are a way to cut through it, not by making the decision cold, but by giving your love and your fear something solid to check themselves against, so that you are deciding from what is real rather than from what you hope or dread.

The Four Anchors

Here is the principle, the last named one in this book. The Four Anchors: whether to build is not decided by how good the good times are, but by four things held together, and when you check them squarely, they point more clearly than any single moment can. Check all four. No single one decides it, but together they cut through the fog.

The first anchor is repair. From the last two chapters, this is the big one. When harm happens, when conflict happens, does it reach repair? Is there accountability, a way back, a pattern that mends rather than only ruptures? A relationship with reliable repair can survive almost anything. A relationship where repair never lands, where ruptures only accumulate, cannot be built on, no matter how good the good days are, because life will keep providing ruptures and you will have no way to mend them.

The second anchor is yourself. Are you still a person in this relationship, or have you disappeared into it? Do you still have your own life, your own needs, your own voice, or have you eroded into the supportive one, the caretaker, the extension of someone else's recovery? A relationship that requires your erasure to function is not a relationship you can build a life in, because there will be no you left to live it. If you have drifted, the question is whether you can come back and still be chosen, or whether your wholeness is treated as a threat.

The third anchor is direction. Not whether things are good right now, but which way they are moving over time. Across months, is the pattern improving, staying flat, or getting worse? Good moments are not the signal, because every relationship has good moments, even ones that are slowly failing. The signal is the trajectory. A hard relationship that is genuinely getting better, slowly, unevenly, but really, is a very different thing from a hard relationship that is getting worse while you tell yourself the good days prove it is fine.

The fourth anchor is their own work. Is your partner engaged in their own healing, in whatever form that takes for them, or are they expecting the relationship, and you, to be the treatment? This is not about whether they are perfectly recovered, which is not the standard and never will be. It is about whether they are doing their part, taking responsibility for their own nervous system and their own growth, rather than outsourcing it to you. A partner working on themselves, however slowly, is a partner you can build with. A partner who expects your love to do the healing for them is offering you a job, not a partnership, and it is a job that has no end.

Reading the anchors together

No single anchor decides this, which is why you hold all four. A relationship can have a rough patch on direction and still be worth building if repair is strong, self is intact, and their own work is real. A relationship can have wonderful good days and still not be worth building if there is no repair, if you have vanished, if it is getting worse, and if they are doing nothing of their own. The point is not to score them and total the points. It is to look at all four plainly, at the same time, and let the whole picture speak, because the whole picture is far more truthful than the last good night or the last bad fight.

Alaris finally used the four anchors and found a mixed but clear answer. Repair was real between them, imperfect but present. Direction was slowly upward. Their partner was doing genuine work of their own. But the second anchor, herself, was the one that had eroded, and when she saw that clearly, the decision was not to leave but to change how she was in it, to come back to her own life and see whether the relationship could hold a whole Alaris rather than a disappearing one. It could. That is one ending. It is not the only one.

Lioren's four anchors told a different story, and he had to be brave enough to read it. He loved his partner, and the good days were genuinely good, and he had built his whole hope on those days. But repair never landed, ruptures only accumulated, the direction over two years was downward, and his partner was doing no work of their own, expecting Lioren's devotion to be the cure. Three anchors were gone and only the good days remained, and the good days, he finally admitted, were not enough to build a life on. He left, and it was one of the hardest and most loving things he ever did, loving toward his partner, whom he stopped asking to be healed by him, and loving toward himself, whom he stopped asking to disappear. Leaving was not a failure of compassion. It was compassion that finally included himself.

The good-days trap

There is a specific reason the direction anchor is so hard to read clearly, and it deserves its own attention, because it traps more people than any other single thing. It is the good days. When your partner is at their best, warm, present, funny, the person you fell for, those days are genuinely wonderful, and they do something dangerous to your judgment. They become the evidence. This is who they really are, you tell yourself, and everything else is just the trauma talking. So you build your assessment of the whole relationship on the peaks and quietly discount the valleys as aberrations.

The trouble is that every relationship has good days, including the ones that are slowly failing. Good days are not rare and they are not proof. A relationship that is getting worse over time still produces good days, sometimes spectacular ones, right up until the end, and if you let the good days set your reading, you will misjudge the trajectory for years. The real question is not how good are the good days. It is what is the actual pattern across all the days, the good and the hard together, and which way is it moving. When you catch yourself building your case on the peaks, gently widen the frame. Count the ordinary days and the hard ones too, and ask what the whole distribution is doing over months. The good days are real, and they are lovely, and they are not, by themselves, an answer.

What does not belong on the list

It helps to name the things people use to decide that are not on the list of four, because these false anchors keep people stuck as reliably as the true ones set them free. How much you have already invested is not an anchor. The months or years you have put in feel like a reason to stay, but they are spent regardless of what you decide, and staying longer to justify having stayed only spends more. How much your partner has suffered is not an anchor. Their pain is real and deserves compassion, but the depth of their history is not a measure of whether this relationship fits your life, and letting it decide for you is how guilt masquerades as love. How much potential you can see is not an anchor either. Who your partner might become if the trauma lifted is a real and moving thing to glimpse, but you cannot build a life with a potential. You can only build one with the person as they actually are, on the actual trajectory they are actually on.

Notice how many of the reasons that keep people in mixed relationships are on this false list rather than the true one. Guilt, sunk cost, sympathy, and hope are powerful, and none of them tells you whether to build. The four anchors do, because they are about what is real and present and moving, not about what you owe or what you have spent or what you can imagine. When you feel the pull of a reason to stay or go, check which list it belongs to. If it is guilt about their suffering or grief over your investment or a vision of their potential, set it gently aside, not because those feelings are wrong, but because they are not the thing that answers the question. Return to the four. Let them, and not the false anchors, be what you decide from.

When you still cannot tell

Sometimes you will run the four anchors in good faith and still not have a clean answer, because one or two of them are genuinely unreadable yet, too early to see the direction, too soon to know whether repair will land, too unclear whether their work is real. This is not a failure of the framework. It is the framework telling you something true, which is that you do not yet have enough information to decide, and that the candid move is not to force a verdict but to keep watching the specific anchor you cannot read.

There is a difference between watching-to-learn and watching-to-avoid, and you have to be clear-eyed with yourself about which one you are doing. Watching-to-learn has a real question and looks for a real answer across a reasonable stretch of time. Watching-to-avoid keeps finding reasons to wait because deciding is frightening, and it can go on for years while the answer sits in plain sight. If the anchors are genuinely unclear, give them fair time to become clear, and set yourself a rough horizon so that watching does not quietly become a way of never choosing. If the anchors are actually clear and you are simply afraid of what they say, that fear is worth naming, because a decision you already know and keep postponing is its own kind of answer.

Leaving can be the loving choice

I want to say this plainly, because trauma-aware people need to hear it more than most. Leaving is sometimes the right and even the loving thing to do, and a trauma history does not obligate you to stay. You are allowed to leave a relationship with someone who has trauma. You are allowed to leave even if they are wounded, even if leaving is hard for them, even if you still love them. Staying out of guilt helps no one, and a relationship you remain in because you are afraid of the harm leaving would cause is not a gift to your partner. It is a slow harm to both of you.

And leaving can be done with care. You can end a relationship cleanly and kindly, without cruelty, without blame, without using your partner's trauma as the reason in a way that wounds them. This relationship is not right for me is a complete sentence, and you do not owe a prosecution of their failures to justify a choice about your own life. Whether you stay and build or leave with care, the decision is yours to make, from your own whole self, and no one, including me, gets to make it for you.

The action: check your four anchors

Here is your work, and it is the culminating one. Take the four anchors, one at a time, and answer each truthfully in writing, because writing resists the fog in a way that thinking does not. Repair: when things go wrong between us, do we find our way back? Self: am I still a whole person in this, or have I disappeared? Direction: over months, is this getting better, flat, or worse? Their work: is my partner doing their own healing, or waiting for me to do it? Do not answer from the last good day, and do not answer from the last bad night. Answer from the pattern, from what has actually been true across time. Then sit with the whole picture, all four together, and let it be as clear or as mixed as it truly is. You may find, like Alaris, that the work is to change how you are in it. You may find, like Lioren, that the loving thing is to go. You may find you need more time to watch an anchor you cannot yet read. Whatever you find, you will have found it from your own whole self, looking at what is real, which is the only place a good decision was ever going to come from. That is the whole aim of this book, and it is where we turn, finally, to close.

Conclusion: A Pace You Both Keep Choosing

Go back to the beginning for a moment, to Avelis in the kitchen, rewriting four months of memories around a single sentence, treating a man she had been laughing with all month like glass. That reflex, the one that takes a fact about trauma and quietly reorganizes a whole relationship around it, was where we started, and everything since has been an argument against it. Not because trauma does not matter. It does. But because the thing trauma actually asks of you is smaller and steadier than the anxious management your first instinct reaches for. It asks you to pay attention to pace, to communicate plainly, to keep yourself, and to stay truthful about what is real. That is the whole book, and it is enough.

Look at what you have now that you did not have at the start. When your partner's trust comes slowly, you have the Pace Principle to remind you that slow is not a verdict on their worth or yours. When you want to reach for their story, you have the Open Door Rule, and you leave the door open instead of pushing it. When the early weeks pull you toward fast fusion, you have the Borrowed Certainty to slow you down, and the Two Whole Lives to keep you a person. When the silence stretches and your mind starts writing the ending, you have the Narrator Trap, and you wait instead of narrating. When closeness is followed by distance, you have the Alarm of Closeness, and you give room instead of chasing. In the body, you have the Living Yes, consent that stays alive. When something gets triggered, you have the Four-Step Pause, and you offer steadiness instead of a fix. When you feel yourself disappearing, you have the Anchor Rule, and you come back. And when the hardest questions arrive, is this a red flag or a trauma response, can we survive conflict, should I stay and build this, you have the Repair Test, the Repair Signal, and the Four Anchors, which do not decide for you but let you decide from what is real.

Notice what none of these tools is. None of them is a way to heal your partner, because that was never your job, and any book that sold you that job was selling you a burden no one can carry. You cannot regulate another person's nervous system. You cannot love someone out of their history. You cannot be the treatment. What you can do is be a steady, open, whole person alongside someone doing their own work, and that turns out to be both less than you feared and more than enough. The relief in that is real. Set down the job you could never do, and pick up the one you actually can.

I want to return, at the end, to the word in the title, because it holds the whole thing. Pace. Not your pace, imposed on your partner until they break. Not their pace, imposed on you until you disappear. A pace you both keep choosing, out loud, on purpose, again and again. That is the difference between a relationship that manages trauma and one that is genuinely shared. The couples in this book who found something real did not find it by one person accommodating the other into oblivion. They found it by negotiating a shared speed, both nervous systems, both sets of needs, both whole lives, and then choosing that speed together, and choosing it again when it drifted. The pace is not something you set once and coast on. It is something you keep choosing, which is also, when you think about it, a decent description of love itself.

And because this was a dating book and not a book about staying no matter what, hold onto the other half of what you learned. Some of the people in these pages stayed and built, and changed how they were in it, and were right to. Some of them left, with care, and were right to. Avelis stopped treating Lorien like glass and found the relationship underneath the trauma. Maevren gave space beautifully for a year and finally admitted she had been calling a wall a wave, and left, and grieved, and was not wrong. Noélin honored a real history and still refused to keep absorbing real harm. Lioren loved someone genuinely and still recognized, when three of his four anchors were gone, that the good days were not a foundation. None of these was a failure of compassion.

Every one of them was a whole person, looking at what was real, and deciding from there. That is all this book ever wanted for you.

So here is where I leave you. You are not your partner's therapist, and you never were. You are a person who cares about someone with a difficult history, and who wants to build something real without rushing, without vanishing, and without pretending. You have the tools now, and more than the tools, you have the frame: notice the pace, communicate plainly, keep yourself, stay truthful, decide. Whatever you decide, and it is genuinely yours to decide, decide it as the whole person you have worked in these pages to stay. That person, present and truthful and still here, is the one who gets to choose. Choose the pace. Keep choosing it. And let the choosing, more than any certainty, be the thing you build on.

References

American Psychiatric Association. (2022). *Diagnostic and statistical manual of mental disorders* (5th ed., text rev.). https://doi.org/10.1176/appi.books.9780890425787

Brewin, C. R., Cloitre, M., Hyland, P., Shevlin, M., Maercker, A., Bryant, R. A., Humayun, A., Jones, L. M., Kagee, A., Rousseau, C., Somasundaram, D., Suzuki, Y., Wessely, S., van Ommeren, M., & Reed, G. M. (2017). A review of current evidence regarding the ICD-11 proposals for diagnosing PTSD and complex PTSD. *Clinical Psychology Review, 58*, 1-15. https://doi.org/10.1016/j.cpr.2017.09.001

Campbell, S. B., & Renshaw, K. D. (2012). Distress in spouses of Vietnam veterans: Associations with communication about deployment experiences. *Journal of Family Psychology, 26*(1), 18-25. https://doi.org/10.1037/a0026680

Cloitre, M., Shevlin, M., Brewin, C. R., Bisson, J. I., Roberts, N. P., Maercker, A., Karatzias, T., & Hyland, P. (2018). The International Trauma Questionnaire: Development of a self-report measure of ICD-11 PTSD and complex PTSD. *Acta Psychiatrica Scandinavica, 138*(6), 536-546. https://doi.org/10.1111/acps.12956

Cook, J. M., Riggs, D. S., Thompson, R., Coyne, J. C., & Sheikh, J. I. (2004). Posttraumatic stress disorder and current relationship functioning among World War II ex-prisoners of war. *Journal of Family Psychology, 18*(1), 36-45. https://doi.org/10.1037/0893-3200.18.1.36

Fredman, S. J., Vorstenbosch, V., Wagner, A. C., Macdonald, A., & Monson, C. M. (2014). Partner accommodation in posttraumatic stress disorder: Initial testing of the Significant Others' Responses to Trauma Scale (SORTS). *Journal of Anxiety Disorders, 28*(4), 372-381. https://doi.org/10.1016/j.janxdis.2014.04.001

Herman, J. L. (1992). *Trauma and recovery: The aftermath of violence from domestic abuse to political terror.* Basic Books.

Leifker, F. R., White, K. H., Blandon, A. Y., & Marshall, A. D. (2015). Posttraumatic stress disorder symptoms impact the emotional experience of intimacy during couple discussions. *Journal of Anxiety Disorders, 29*, 119-127. https://doi.org/10.1016/j.janxdis.2014.11.005

Mikulincer, M., & Shaver, P. R. (2016). *Attachment in adulthood: Structure, dynamics, and change* (2nd ed.). Guilford Press.

Monk, J. K., & Nelson Goff, B. S. (2014). Military couples' trauma disclosure: Moderating between trauma symptoms and relationship quality. *Psychological Trauma: Theory, Research, Practice, and Policy, 6*(5), 537-545. https://doi.org/10.1037/a0036788

Monson, C. M., & Fredman, S. J. (2012). *Cognitive-behavioral conjoint therapy for PTSD: Harnessing the healing power of relationships.* Guilford Press.

National Center for PTSD. (n.d.). *PTSD and the family.* U.S. Department of Veterans Affairs. https://www.ptsd.va.gov/professional/treat/specific/ptsd_family.asp

Shevlin, M., Hyland, P., Roberts, N. P., Bisson, J. I., Brewin, C. R., & Cloitre, M. (2018). A psychometric assessment of disturbances in self-organization symptom indicators for ICD-11 complex PTSD using the International Trauma Questionnaire. *European Journal of Psychotraumatology, 9*(1), 1419749. https://doi.org/10.1080/20008198.2017.1419749

van der Kolk, B. A. (2014). *The body keeps the score: Brain, mind, and body in the healing of trauma.* Viking.

World Health Organization. (2019). *International classification of diseases for mortality and morbidity statistics* (11th ed.). https://icd.who.int/

About the Author

Lawrence Simeon Mooney writes about relationships, trauma, and the ordinary decisions that shape them. This book grew out of a simple observation: almost every guide for partners of trauma survivors assumes a marriage worth saving, and almost none of them speak to the person who is still deciding whether to build something at all.